Advance Praise for

MEDIA LITERACY IS ELEMENTARY

"Not teaching critical media literacy to your first graders? Why not?! With television and Internet content shaping how children see their world and themselves, Jeff Share argues 'the earlier the better.' This book makes a compelling case for helping our youngest students analyze and create media. Taking up the tools—cameras, computers, pens, and pencils—in their own hands, children begin to participate in the discourse of democracy. Most importantly, they learn that they belong."

Carol Jago, Vice President of the National Council of Teachers of English;
Director of the California Reading and Literature Project at UCLA

"Media literacy needs to be understood as a fundamental component of any well-rounded educational curriculum in the twenty-first century. In this groundbreaking work, Jeff Share argues persuasively that it is never too early to help young children learn the skills they need to make sense of the media culture in which they're already immersed. Quite simply, this book should be required reading for all elementary educators, administrators, educational policy makers, and parents too."

Jackson Katz, Creator of the educational video
Tough Guise: Violence, Media and the Crisis in Masculinity

MEDIA
LITERACY
IS
ELEMENTARY

Rethinking Childhood

Joe L. Kincheloe and Gaile Cannella
General Editors

Vol. 41

PETER LANG
New York • Washington, D.C./Baltimore • Bern
Frankfurt am Main • Berlin • Brussels • Vienna • Oxford

Jeff Share

MEDIA
LITERACY
IS
ELEMENTARY

Teaching Youth to Critically Read and Create Media

PETER LANG
New York • Washington, D.C./Baltimore • Bern
Frankfurt am Main • Berlin • Brussels • Vienna • Oxford

Library of Congress Cataloging-in-Publication Data

Share, Jeff.
Critical media is elementary: teaching youth to critically read
and create media / Jeff Share.
p. cm. — (Rethinking childhood; v. 41)
Includes bibliographical references.
1. Media literacy. 2. Mass media—Study and teaching (Elementary).
3. Mass media criticism. I. Title.
P96.M4S53   372.67'2—dc22   2008028251
ISBN 978-1-4331-0402-2 (hardcover)
ISBN 978-1-4331-0392-6 (paperback)
ISSN 1086-7155

Bibliographic information published by **Die Deutsche Bibliothek**
Die Deutsche Bibliothek lists this publication in the "Deutsche
Nationalbibliografie"; detailed bibliographic data is available
on the Internet at http://dnb.ddb.de/.

Chart on page 142 © 2002 Center for Media Literacy, www.medialit.org

Cover design by Oliver Kish

The paper in this book meets the guidelines for permanence and durability
of the Committee on Production Guidelines for Book Longevity
of the Council of Library Resources.

© 2009 Peter Lang Publishing, Inc., New York
29 Broadway, 18th floor, New York, NY 10006
www.peterlang.com

Printed in the United States of America

This book is dedicated to my family who has always supported me to follow my dreams and encouraged me to work for social justice.

Contents

Preface

by Douglas Kellner

Jeff Share has long been an advocate of teaching critical media literacy to children and seen the importance of making media studies an essential part of education from K-12 through the university level. An award-winning photojournalist whose work appeared in *Life*, *Time*, *Newsweek* and many other publications, Share turned to public school teaching on the elementary school level when he became disillusioned with journalism. Teaching a bilingual fourth grade class at Leo Politi Elementary School in downtown Los Angeles, Share began integrating media literacy concepts into his core curriculum. He taught his students how to look critically at images and the media that surrounds them. His students also became media makers and used cameras as tools to communicate their ideas and concerns with people outside their classroom. Share's fourth-graders explored their community, their cultures and their mediated lives as hands-on social studies researchers and language arts reporters. After six years of teaching, Share left the classroom to work on Project SMARTArt (Students using Media, Art, Reading, and Technology), a federal grant, training 23 teachers and artists at Leo Politi Elementary School from 2001 to 2004.

After these years of teaching media literacy in the trenches of public schools, Share decided to get his Ph.D. at UCLA in 2003 and I happily took him on as a student. Not surprisingly, Share wrote his Ph.D. dissertation on Critical Media Literacy, which was concluded in 2006. During this time, we published several articles on critical media literacy including "Critical Media Literacy, Democracy, and the Reconstruction of Education," *Media Literacy. A Reader*, edited by Donald Macedo and Shirley R. Steinberg (2007).

Drawing on his Ph.D. research and further theoretical reflections on media literacy, Share has been developing his investigations into how to engage children and teach them critical media literacy. At the same time, he has been engaged in critical media literacy training exercises with students and teachers, and making presentations on critical media literacy at many schools and conferences, while writing up his research and ideas in this book. Share focuses on the literacies and pedagogies necessary to teach critical media literacy to young students on the K-12 level and to empower students and citizens to becoming media literate and active participants in their society. Students can then become teachers and citizens, helping their peers, teachers, and parents understand media and become media literate, while using media to express themselves and transform their society and culture.

Using the case study of Project SMARTArt, Share returns to the teachers he trained and questions them about their experiences and thoughts regarding teaching media literacy in elementary school. The teachers share anecdotes, articulate many fascinating ideas about teaching media literacy and express their frustrations about the current challenges they face in the age of back-to-basics and high-stakes testing. The lack of research and literature of media education in the primary grades make Share's investigation even more meaningful.

In particular, Share explores in this book the potential of teaching critical media literacy to young children from preschool to first grade, between the ages of 3 and 7. While critical media literacy is a subject that is seldom considered with young students, Share argues that it is essential for educators to begin teaching critical thinking and media literacy as early as possible, especially in relation to topics of media and democracy and social justice. Since the first public pedagogy that most children encounter comes right into their own homes and surrounds them in society in the form of cartoons, songs, toys, food packaging, clothing, home decorations, and so on, Share proposes that social researchers should investigate the best ways to help students understand and negotiate these multimodal messages, ubiquitous media and consumer culture, and new information communication technologies.

Share argues that critical teachers need skills to help them question and understand the highly constructed mass mediated messages that are too often embraced as merely entertainment, all the while positioning, framing and shaping the viewer's perceptions of her/his self and world. Exploring classroom examples of work in critical literacy and multimedia literacy with children from preschool on up, Share frames his interpretation of their work within the context of theoretical work by Carmen Luke, Alan Luke, Stuart Hall, Peter Freebody, Paulo Freire, Douglas Kellner, David Buckingham, Marsha Kinder, and others. His inquiry aims to expose theoretical as well as practical possibilities for building some of the first steps toward critical media literacy with young children.

The studies in this book thus show some ways that teachers can teach critical media literacy, illustrating both positive pedagogies and the challenges that teachers face, especially with difficult issues of decoding media representations of sensitive topics like gender, race, class, and sexuality. Share frames his own conception of teaching critical media literacy within the context of Freirean critical pedagogy and aiming at social justice. Share's analysis is also Deweyan in that it promotes education for democracy and calls for a reconstruction of education to help create a more democratic society.

CHAPTER ONE

Introduction

> A media culture has emerged in which images, sounds, and spectacles help produce
> the fabric of everyday life, dominating leisure time, shaping political views and social
> behavior, and providing the materials out of which people forge their very identities.
> (Kellner, 1995, p. 1)

The world we live in today is very different from the one that most of us remember from our childhood. The 21st century is a media-saturated, technologically dependent, and globally connected world. However, most education in the U.S. has not kept up with advances in technology or educational research. In our global information society, it is insufficient and irresponsible to teach students to read and write only with letters and numbers. We live in a multimedia age where the majority of information people receive comes less often from print sources and more typically from highly constructed visual images, complex sound arrangements, and multiple media formats. Almost every U.S. household has at least one television set[1] over half have computers with Internet access. In just the last decade there has been an enormous growth in the availability and use of new information communication technologies, from smart phones with video capabilities and web access to computers that can

network people around the world for playing virtual games or organizing social movements. In the conclusion to the Kaiser Family Foundation's national
study of media usage of 8–18 year olds, the authors assert, "Without question,
this generation truly is the media generation, devoting more than a quarter of
each day to media" (Rideout, Roberts & Foehr, 2005, p. 39).

Who to admire, how to solve problems, what to think about groups of
people you have never met, when and how to have sex, where to find what
you need, and why care about others are just some of the lessons that children
are receiving daily from the mass media. The influential role media play in
organizing, shaping, and disseminating information, ideas, and values is creating a powerful *public pedagogy* (Giroux, 1999; Luke, 1997). Shirley Steinberg
and Joe Kincheloe write, "In the late twentieth and early twenty-first centuries
corporate-produced children's culture has replaced schooling as the producer
of the central curriculum of childhood" (2004, p. 11). Today's storytellers are
enormous transnational corporations merging and expanding internationally
to just about every corner of the globe and domestically to every nook and
cranny they can reach. Today, fewer than 10 corporations own the majority of
the world's media, creating a small group of wealthy people with tremendous
power to decide who and what will be represented and what lessons will be
taught by the largest cultural industry the world has ever known (McChesney,
2003).

When a small group of people has the power to create and disseminate
enormous amounts of information, the diversity of ideas shrinks as the potential for abuse increases. Media consolidation is especially problematic when the
majority of the audience perceives media messages as neutral and transparent.
This positivist perspective supports an unproblematic relationship with media
in which these messages are rarely questioned or challenged. Critical inquiry,
therefore, becomes an essential requirement for literacy in the 21st century.
Changes in technology, media, and society require the development of critical media literacy to empower students and citizens to adequately read media
messages and produce media themselves in order to be active participants in a
democratic society (Kellner, 1995; Kellner & Share, 2005).

Much of the daily public pedagogy that mass media teach about race, gender, class, sexuality, consumption, fear, morals, and the like reflect corporate
profit motives at the expense of social concerns necessary for a healthy and
vibrant democracy. Since traditional education does not provide the tools to
help students recognize and counteract these influences, we need a new type of
literacy that *expands* to encompass new information communication technologies (ICTs), media, and popular culture, and that *deepens* pedagogical practices

to more complex levels of critical analysis. Through a horizontal expansion of literacy and a vertical deepening of critical inquiry, critical media literacy aims to challenge popular assumptions that frame media as unproblematic windows to the world. An essential concept of media literacy is the social construction of knowledge and the ramifications of that understanding to disrupt positivist misconceptions (Kellner & Share, 2007).

Since mass media are usurping other cultural and socializing forces such as books, families, schools, churches, and so on, Douglas Kellner stresses the need for a new type of pedagogy. He writes,

> A critical media pedagogy develops concepts and analyses that will enable readers to critically dissect the artifacts of contemporary media and consumer culture, help them to unfold the meanings and effects on their culture, and thus give individuals power over their cultural environment. (1995, p. 10)

This new pedagogical approach to literacy offers the dual possibility of resisting media domination through critical analysis and empowering individuals to create alternative media for counterhegemonic expression. Available online for free is a set of 25 lesson plans I wrote to help teachers integrate media literacy into their instruction.[2]

In the next chapter, different theoretical approaches to media education are reviewed, and a framework for critical media literacy, built largely on cultural studies and critical pedagogy, is proposed. Through analyzing different approaches to media education, the key elements necessary for critical media literacy become more apparent. Focusing on social justice and issues of power are prime concerns of critical media literacy, and they are the main elements that separate critical media literacy from the more positivist media literacy movement in the U.S.

In Chapter Three, the current situation of media education in the U.S. is assessed and a couple of exceptional examples of critical media literacy are highlighted. While the U.S. is the largest producer of mass media, there is sadly little media education occurring in the majority of U.S. schools. However, the groundwork is being laid for a new era of educators to take up the cause of bringing media literacy into U.S. education. Two after-school programs, one in New York and one in Los Angeles, provide outstanding examples of what is possible. Some interesting media education occurring outside the U.S. is also presented.

This general analysis of media education is followed by a specific case study in Chapter Four in which interviews with a group of elementary school teachers shed light onto the difficult task of teaching media literacy in the current conservative era of skills-based education driven by high-stakes testing. At the beginning of the 21st century, the U.S. Department of Education and the National Endowment for the Arts funded 17 demonstration projects across the country to integrate media literacy with the arts. Based at the Leo Politi Elementary School in downtown Los Angeles, Project SMARTArt (Students using Media, Art, Reading, and Technology) was one of the largest grant recipients. For 3 years, students from kindergarten to fifth grade worked with teachers and artists to analyze media and create their own alternative representations of everything from violence to advertising to their community. Students produced animation, performed original plays, painted, wrote, photographed, and used numerous types of media to analyze and communicate, read, and write their world.

At Leo Politi Elementary School, I trained the 23 teachers who participated in the grant. I met regularly with them in groups and in one-on-one coaching sessions, and I modeled media literacy lessons with their students. A case study about this project is available online with photographs, videos, and lesson plans.[3] The grant ended in 2004 and most of the teachers are still teaching, but little is known about what effects the 3 years of media literacy training and support had on their teaching practices.

These elementary school teachers provide fascinating insight into their situation at a low performing inner-city school that received federal funding to engage with media literacy. While all these teachers believe in the need for teaching media literacy, most are now struggling to find the time or freedom necessary to continue teaching it like they used to when they were receiving the federal money. Chapter Four provides a qualitative assessment of the impact Project SMARTArt has had on the project teachers' pedagogical practices and beliefs. The goal of this inquiry is not to evaluate this specific project; rather it aims to reveal from practicing elementary school teachers what they have found are some of the best ways to teach critical media literacy.

One of the many interesting issues that arose from their interviews was the question of developmental appropriateness of critical media literacy with elementary school-age children. For this reason, in Chapter Five I compare and contrast two exemplary educators teaching young children from 3 to 6 years of age. One teacher, working in a bilingual charter school in Los Angeles, demonstrates wonderful work with her kindergarten and first-grade students using technology and creating media. The other teacher, working at a suburban preschool in Toronto, Canada, demonstrates amazing success teaching young children about social justice through a problem-posing pedagogy. These teachers demonstrate important elements necessary for critical media literacy to become more inclusive of different media and technology as well as more critical in analyzing issues of power and taking action against injustice.

The final chapter (Chapter Six) looks at some of the latest changes in society that have created the pressing need for a different type of education that will address these issues. Changes in technology and global capitalism have reshaped societies across the globe. These are changes that can be powerful tools for creating new democratic possibilities or dangerous weapons to control and oppress millions of people and exploit the earth's limited resources. Much is at stake, and it is no longer acceptable to allow protectionist fears of media or blind adoration for it to keep educators from teaching students the citizenship skills of critical analysis and production that they need to fully participate and shape democracy in the 21st century.

CHAPTER TWO

Teaching the Media

Competing Approaches, Media Activism, and Core Concepts of Critical Media Literacy

The traditional ideas of literacy that focus on a standard national language and phonetic decoding are no longer sufficient in an age of countless communication systems and increasing linguistic and cultural diversity (The New London Group, 1996). The psychological model of reading and writing as individual cognitive skills needs to evolve to a deeper sociological understanding of literacy as a social practice "tied up in the politics and power relations of everyday life in literate cultures" (Luke & Freebody, 1997, p. 185).

Current methods of representation are profuse and evolving as technology develops and spreads. These changes in technology and society have led to a call for a broader approach to literacy by an international group of educators who refer to themselves as The New London Group.[1] They propose a pedagogy of "multiliteracies" to address the different types of representation, much more extensively than traditional print-based approaches. They also suggest that the growing local, cultural, and linguistic diversity, along with global connectedness, require a new literacy pedagogy that can meet these multiple demands. They write, "The role of pedagogy is to develop an epistemology of pluralism that provides access without people having to erase or leave behind different subjectivities" (1996, p. 72). The New London Group's concept of multiliteracies helps students negotiate multiple cultural and linguistic differences as well as the multitude of communication media. They suggest that media literacy is one of the many literacies that students need in the 21st century to participate more effectively in the democratic process.

This chapter explores the theoretical underpinnings of critical media literacy, examines some of the obstacles for implementing progressive pedagogical changes, and provides examples of practical applications. A multiperspectival approach addressing issues of gender, race, class, and power is used to explore the interconnections of media literacy, cultural studies, and critical pedagogy.

Different Approaches to Media Education

In spite of the fact that media education in the U.S. is in its infancy, there is already debate about *why* and *how* to teach it (Hobbs, 1998; Tyner, 1998). Kellner (1998) divides the field of media pedagogy into four general approaches in order to better explain the necessary elements of critical media literacy.

One approach to media education emerges from a fear of media and aims to protect or inoculate people against the dangers of media manipulation and addiction. This *protectionist approach* posits media audiences as passive victims and values traditional print culture over media culture as exemplified by Neil Postman (1985) in *Amusing Ourselves to Death*. Postman warns that TV has become a powerful force of pedagogy that dominates the attention, time, and cognitive habits of youth. Many activists on both sides of the political spectrum come to media education as a way to push their agenda through blaming the media. Some conservatives blame the media for causing teen pregnancies and the destruction of family values while some liberals blame the media for rampant consumerism and making children materialistic. From her research with preschool teachers/child care providers, Ellen Seiter (2002) found this fear of media and popular culture greatest at middle- and upper-class economic levels. She writes, "the media are deemed most powerful by those working and living in situations of relative privilege; in the poorest centre the media are seen as only one factor—less significant than the part played by poverty, by parental absence, and by violence" (pp. 59–60).

Although it is important to recognize that media can contribute to and at times cause many social problems, at issue with this approach is its decontextualization and antimedia bias that oversimplify the complexity of our relationship with media. A protectionist stance also takes away the potential for empowerment that critical pedagogy and alternative media production offer. When the understanding of media effects is contextualized within their social and historical dynamics, then issues of representation and ideology are extremely useful to media education to explore the interconnections between media and society, information, and power (Ferguson, 1998, 2004). Critics of this antimedia approach suggest that it will cause students to either regurgitate "politically correct" responses to media critique or reject the ideas of media literacy altogether (Buckingham, 1994). Aspects of a protectionist approach can be useful when they address the naturalizing processes of ideology and the interrelationships with social injustice, but it is deeply flawed when it does so through dogmatic orthodoxy and undemocratic pedagogy.

A second approach to teaching about media can be seen in *media arts education* where students are taught to value the aesthetic qualities of media and the arts while using their creativity for self-expression through creating art and media. These programs can be found most often inside schools as stand-alone classes or outside of the classroom in community-based or after-school programs. Many of these programs are excellent examples of critical media literacy as described in Chapter Three. However, they can be problematic when they favor individualistic self-expression over socially conscious analysis and alternative media production. Many media arts programs unproblematically teach students the technical skills to merely reproduce hegemonic representations with little awareness of ideological implications or any type of social critique. Feminist standpoint theorists explain that coming to voice is important for people who have seldom been allowed to speak for themselves, but without critical analysis, it is not enough (Collins, 2004; Harding, 2004; Hartsock, 1997). Critical analysis that explores and exposes the structures of oppression is essential because merely coming to voice is something any racist or sexist group of people can also claim. Spaces must be opened up and opportunities created so that people in marginalized positions have the opportunity to collectively struggle against oppression, to voice their concerns, and to create their own representations.

Incorporating the arts and media production into public school education offers the potential for making learning more experiential, hands-on, creative, expressive, and fun. The arts also bring an aesthetic component to education, something that is often overlooked or downplayed as unimportant. According to Ray Mission and Wendy Morgan (2006), by engaging aesthetics in education, teachers can create new opportunities for students to access different truths, provide a broad range of personal development, and make learning more fulfilling and entertaining. They write, "The aesthetic may only be one among many ways of knowing that human beings have, but it is a significant one because it acknowledges the breadth, diversity, and even contradictoriness of human experiences, as well as the drive to make sense of it" (p. 226).

Media arts education can bring aesthetics, pleasure, and popular culture into mainstream education, thereby making schools more motivating, diverse, and relevant to students. When this approach moves beyond technical production skills or relativist art appreciation and is steeped in cultural studies and critical pedagogy that address issues of gender, race, class, sexuality, and power, it holds dramatic potential for transformative critical media literacy.

A third approach to media education can be found in the *media literacy movement* in the U.S. While the movement is relatively small,[2] it has made some inroads into mainstream educational institutions and has established two national membership organizations in the U.S. According to the definition of media literacy provided by one of the two national media literacy organizations, the National Association for Media Literacy Education (NAMLE), "media literacy is seen to consist of a series of communication competencies, including the ability to ACCESS, ANALYZE, EVALUATE and COMMUNICATE."[3] This approach attempts to expand the notion of literacy to include popular culture and multiple forms of media (music, film, video, Internet, advertising, etc.) while still working within a print literacy tradition (Kellner, 1998).

A major advantage that this approach offers public education is its expansion of literacy and its inclusion of popular culture as worthy of serious study. Anne Haas Dyson (1997) writes that children have agency to appropriate cultural material and are attracted to popular media. She warns, "If official curricula make no space for this agency, then schools risk reinforcing societal divisions in children's orientations to each other, to cultural art forms, and, to school itself" (p. 181). Regardless of the teacher's desires, mass media seep into the classroom either discreetly by students smuggling toys in their backpacks or overtly as cartoon characters blazoned across everything from clothing to food packaging. The love affair that elementary school students have with mass media is seldom more obvious than on each Valentine's Day when millions of tiny hands across the U.S. distribute their commercially produced valentine cards, donning their favorite media characters and prepackaged words of adoration. Teachers who take a protectionist stance against children's media and try to censor or prohibit its entry into the school are not only fighting an uphill battle, but they are also losing a tremendous opportunity to connect education to their students' personal experiences and teach critical thinking in a meaningful context. Popular culture and mass media are part of the experiences that students bring with them to school and should be embraced and critiqued within the formal educational curricula.

Typically referred to as media literacy education, the ideas behind this approach are sometimes connected to information literacy, technology literacy, multimodal literacy, and other attempts to broaden print literacy concepts to include different tools and modes of communicating. It is important to begin with these ideas of expanding our understanding of how we communicate with more than just printed words. However, this is not enough to bring about a democratic reconstruction of education and society. Robert Ferguson (1998) uses the metaphor of an iceberg to explain the need for critical media analysis. Many educators working under an apolitical media literacy framework guide their students to analyze only the obvious and overt tip of the iceberg they see sticking out of the water. Ferguson asserts that this is a problem because "The vast bulk which is not immediately visible is the intellectual, historical and analytical base without which media analysis runs the risk of becoming superficial, mechanical or glib" (p. 2). The critical component of media literacy must transform literacy education into an exploration of the role of language and communication to define relationships of power and domination because below the surface of that iceberg lies deeply embedded ideological notions of white supremacy, capitalist patriarchy, classism, homophobia, and other oppressive myths. Carlos Cortés complains that a problem with much media literacy material is that they "only tangentially or incidentally touch upon questions of diversity" (2000, p. 142).

Many media literacy educators working from this approach openly express the belief that education can and should be politically neutral and that their job is to objectively expose students to media content without questioning ideology or issues of power. Giroux writes, "The notion that theory, facts, and inquiry can be objectively determined and used falls prey to a set of values that are both conservative and mystifying in their political orientation" (1997, p. 11).

The mainstream appeal of the media literacy movement, something that is only just starting to develop in the U.S., can probably be linked to its conservative base that does not engage the political dimensions of education, especially literacy. While this ambiguous nonpartisan stance helps the dissemination of media education, thereby making some of the ideas available to more students, it also waters down the transformative potential for media education to become a powerful tool to challenge oppression and strengthen democracy. The media literacy movement has done excellent work in promoting important concepts of semiotics and intertextuality, as well as in bringing popular culture into public education. However, without critical pedagogy and cultural studies, media literacy risks becoming another cookbook of conventional ideas that only improve the social reproductive function of education.

The type of *critical media literacy* that Douglas Kellner and I propose (Kellner & Share, 2005) includes aspects of the three previous models, but focuses on ideology critique and analyzing the politics of representation of crucial dimensions of gender, race, class, and sexuality; incorporating alternative media production; and expanding textual analysis to include issues of social context, control, resistance, and pleasure. A critical media literacy approach also expands literacy to include information literacy, technical literacy, multimodal literacy, and other attempts to broaden print literacy concepts to include different tools and modes of communicating (Kellner, 1998). In addition to these elements, critical media literacy brings an understanding of ideology, power, and domination that challenges relativist and apolitical notions of media education in order to guide teachers and students in their explorations of how power and information are always linked. This approach embraces the notion of the audience as active in the process of making meaning, as a cultural struggle between dominant readings, oppositional readings, and negotiated readings (Ang, 2002; Hall, 1980).

Critical media literacy thus constitutes a critique of mainstream approaches to literacy and a political project for democratic social change. This involves a multiperspectival critical inquiry, of popular culture and the cultural industries, that addresses issues of class, race, gender, sexuality, and power and also promotes the production of alternative counterhegemonic media. Media and information communication technologies can be tools for empowerment when people who are most often marginalized or misrepresented in the mainstream media receive the opportunity to use these tools to tell their stories and express their concerns. For members of the dominant group, critical media literacy offers an opportunity to engage with the social realities that the majority of the world is experiencing and understand the interconnections that link the globally networked society. The new technologies of communication are powerful tools that can liberate or dominate, manipulate or enlighten, and it is imperative that educators teach their students how to use and critically analyze the new tools of the information age (Kellner, 2004).

The different approaches to media education are not rigid pedagogical models as much as they are interpretive reference points from which educators frame their concerns, goals, and strategies. Calling for critical media literacy is important to identify the elements and objectives necessary for good media pedagogy.

Alan Luke and Peter Freebody (1997) have been developing a dynamic understanding of literacy as social practices where critical competence is one of the necessary practices. This sociological framing of literacy as a *family of prac-*

tices in which multiple practices are crucial and none alone is enough fits well into a multiperspectival approach to critical media literacy. Luke and Freebody (1999) write that effective literacy requires four basic roles that allow learners to "break the code . . . participate in understanding and composing . . . use texts functionally . . . [and] critically analyze and transform texts by acting on knowledge that texts are not ideologically natural or neutral." This normative approach offers the flexibility for literacy education to explore and critically engage students with the pedagogy that will work best for each teacher in his or her own unique situation with the different social and cultural needs and interests of his or her students and local community.

When educators teach students critical media literacy, they often begin with media arts activities or simple decoding of media texts in the mode of the established media literacy movement with discussion of how audiences receive media messages. But critical media literacy also engages students in exploring the depths of the iceberg with critical questions to challenge "commonsense" assumptions and redesign alternative media arts production with negotiated and oppositional interpretations. The goal should be to move toward critical media literacy with the understanding of literacy as a social process that requires breadth and depth, while planting seeds and scaffolding the steps for transformative pedagogy.

For example, in her course on critical media literacy at UCLA, Rhonda Hammer has her students work in teams to create their own counterhegemonic movies and Web sites that explore issues they feel are underrepresented or misrepresented in mainstream media (see Hammer, 2006).[4] During the short 10-week quarter, her students produce movies and Web sites that challenge the commonsense assumptions about a wide assortment of issues dealing with gender, ethnicity, sexuality, politics, power, and pleasure. Through the dialectic of theory and practice, her students create critical alternative media while engaging the core concepts of critical media literacy as they apply to audience, text, and context.

Social Activism and Media Production

David Buckingham (2000) suggests that young people are alienated and disenfranchised from politics because they "are not defined in our society as political subjects, let alone as political agents" (p. 219). He suggests that teachers, as well as journalists, need "to find ways of establishing the *relevance* of politics and of *connecting* the 'micro-politics' of personal experience with the 'macropolitics' of the public sphere" (p. 221). The path Buckingham promotes requires a type of media education that encourages "young people's *critical participation* as cultural producers in their own right" (p. 222). The importance for youth to create media is something that Nick Couldry suggests applies to more than just news and nonfiction. He writes, "The ability to participate in the production of shared fictions remains fundamental to any sense of belonging, and therefore to 'citizenship' and 'identity' themselves" (2000, p. 194). New ICTs hold tremendous potential for empowering youth to become critical participators like Buckingham and Couldry mention; however, these new tools are not the great panacea that some like Sherry Turkle (1997) fetishize. After working with youth in an after-school program in which students produced their own community newspaper, Ellen Seiter found that the Internet was more of an impediment to politicizing students and issues than a beneficial tool for consciousness raising. Seiter explains that now kids are learning technology after it has "been thoroughly colonized by the entertainment industries" (2004, p. 103). She writes, "the massive commercialization of the web and its energetic targeting of elementary school children will make the more intellectually challenging uses of the internet a profound challenge in the school environment" (p. 105). That same problem exists for the home environment as well.

The manner in which most media cloak their role in reproducing hegemony as merely entertainment or information tends to hamper critical analysis of the inequalities of power in society and in our relationships with media. Couldry argues

> that it is in part *through* the many processes by which the media are absorbed into everyday social life (including the pleasures they generate) that an additional level of social inequality is entrenched: the inequality between those with greater access to the media's symbolic power and those with less. (p. 21)

If one believes that media production has the potential to politicize youth, then much of children's media production could be seen as cultivating future participative citizenship. While most children's interactions with media production are not political and rarely critical, they can become steps along the empowerment process that Paulo Freire (1970) discusses in the movement from being an object that is acted upon to becoming an empowered subject. As students create their own media, they have the opportunity to disrupt adult authorial power and position themselves as the creators of new media messages in their own voices and from their own perspectives.

Critical media literacy in this conception is tied to the project of radical democracy and is concerned with developing skills that will enhance democratization and civic participation. It takes a comprehensive approach that teaches critical skills and how to use media as instruments of social communication and change. The technologies of communication are becoming more and more accessible to young people and ordinary citizens and can be used to promote education, democratic self-expression, and social progress. Technologies that could help produce the end of participatory democracy, by transforming politics into media spectacles and the battle of images, and by turning spectators into passive consumers, could also be used to help invigorate democratic debate and participation (Kellner, 1995).

Indeed, teaching critical media literacy should be a participatory, collaborative project. Watching television shows or films together could promote productive discussions between teachers and students (or parents and children), with emphasis on eliciting student views, producing a variety of interpretations of media texts, and teaching basic principles of hermeneutics and criticism. Students are often more media savvy, knowledgeable, and immersed in media culture than their teachers, and they can contribute to the educational process through sharing their ideas, perceptions, and insights. Along with critical discussion, debate, and analysis, teachers ought to be guiding students in an inquiry process that deepens their critical exploration of issues that affect them and society. Since media culture is often part and parcel of students' identity and a most powerful cultural experience, teachers must be sensitive in criticizing artifacts and perceptions that students hold dear, yet an atmosphere of critical respect for difference and inquiry into the nature and effects of media culture should be promoted (Luke, 1997).

A major challenge in developing critical media literacy, however, results from the fact that it is not a pedagogy in the traditional sense with firmly established principles, a canon of texts, and tried-and-true teaching procedures. It requires a democratic pedagogy that involves teachers sharing power with students as they join together in the process of unveiling myths, challenging hegemony, and searching for methods of producing their own alternative media. Critical media pedagogy in the U.S. is in its infancy; it is just beginning to produce results and is more open and experimental than established print-oriented pedagogy.

Teaching critical media literacy requires an approach that is neither fearfully protectionist nor blindly celebratory. One can teach how media culture provides significant statements or insights about the social world, empowering visions of gender, race, and class or complex aesthetic structures and practices, thereby putting a positive spin on how it can provide significant contributions to education. Yet, media culture can also advance sexism, racism, ethnocentrism, homophobia, and other forms of prejudice, as well as misinformation, problematic ideologies, and questionable values. The complexity of media culture and the different possibilities for media education require critical media educators to promote a dialectical approach to media.

Core Concepts of Critical Media Literacy

While media education has evolved from many disciplines, an important arena of theoretical work for critical media literacy comes from the multidisciplinary field of cultural studies. This is a field of critical inquiry that began over a century ago in Europe and continues to grow with new critiques of media and society. From the 1930s through the 1960s, researchers at the Frankfurt Institute for Social Research used critical social theory to analyze how popular culture and the new tools of communication technology induce ideology and social control. In the 1960s, researchers at the Centre for Contemporary Cultural Studies at the University of Birmingham added to the earlier concerns of ideology with a more sophisticated understanding of the audience as active makers of meaning, not simply mirrors of an external reality. Applying concepts of semiotics, feminism, multiculturalism, and postmodernism, a dialectical understanding of political economy, textual analysis, and audience theory has evolved in which media and popular culture can be analyzed as dynamic discourses that reproduce dominant ideologies as well as entertain, educate, and offer possibilities for counterhegemonic alternatives (Kellner, 1995).

In the 1980s, cultural studies research began to enter the educational arena. With the publication of Len Masterman's *Teaching the Media* (1985/2001), many educators around the world embraced media education less as a specific body of knowledge or set of skills and more as a framework of *conceptual understandings* (Buckingham, 2003). Various people and organizations across the globe have generated, and continue to create, different lists of media literacy concepts[5] that vary in numbers and wording, but for the most tend to coincide with at least five basic elements:

1. recognition of the construction of media and communication as a social process as opposed to accepting texts as isolated neutral or transparent conveyors of information;
2. some type of textual analysis that explores the languages, genres, aesthetics, codes, and conventions of the text;
3. exploration of the role audiences play in actively negotiating meanings;
4. problematizing the process of representation to uncover and engage

issues of ideology, power, and pleasure;

5. examination of the production, institutions, and political economy that motivate and structure the media industries as corporate profit-seeking businesses.

By the late 1980s, a group of high school English teachers in Ontario, Canada, created a list of eight *Key Concepts* that meshed their experiences in literature analysis with cultural studies to produce a pedagogical framework to deconstruct media texts. Based on their work, the Ontario Ministry of Education published these eight key concepts of media literacy:

1. All media are constructions.
2. The media construct reality.
3. Audiences negotiate meaning in media.
4. Media have commercial implications.
5. Media contain ideological and value messages.
6. Media have social and political implications.
7. Form and content are closely related in the media.
8. Each medium has a unique aesthetic form.[6]

During this same time, the British Film Institute developed a list of six *Signpost Questions* for students to focus on when analyzing a media text:

WHO is communicating with whom?	AGENCIES
WHAT type of text is it?	CATEGORIES
HOW is it produced?	TECHNOLOGIES
HOW do we know what it means?	LANGUAGES
WHO receives it and what sense do they make of it?	AUDIENCES
HOW does it present its subject?	REPRESENTATIONS[7]

While much was happening internationally in media education, the world's leading producer of media, the U.S., has been far behind. In the U.S., the Center for Media Literacy (CML) took many of the foundational concepts of media education that evolved from educators and academics in various parts of the world working in the fields of cultural studies, media theory, literature analysis, and critical pedagogy and developed a simplified list of five core concepts and corresponding questions for adults and young children (see Appendix A).[8] The goal of this framework is to make teaching media literacy easier and more accessible to K-12 educators. The CML framework is an inquiry-based process that begins with *Five Key Questions* developed to assist students to explore the *Five Core Concepts* of media literacy. The CML framework was the primary theoretical tool used for Project SMARTArt.

In an attempt to maintain some of the pragmatic simplicity of CML's framework while strengthening its critical component, with the help of Douglas Kellner and others, I created a modified list of conceptual understandings and prompts for teaching critical media literacy (see Appendix B).

Understanding the elements of different approaches to media education is important for recognizing various strategies, objectives, benefits, and limitations. However, to be able to teach media literacy, it is essential to understand the core concepts. The following is an explanation of the theory behind each of the five core concepts used during Project SMARTArt and examples of implementation.

Core Concept #1: Principle of Non-transparency

All Media Messages Are "Constructed"

The first core concept is the foundation of media literacy, which challenges the power of media to present messages as nonproblematic and transparent. Since messages are created by people who make decisions about what to communicate and how to communicate, all messages are influenced by the subjectivity and biases of those creating the message as well as the social contexts within which the process occurs. Along with this encoding subjectivity comes the multiple readings of the text as it is decoded by various audiences in different contexts. Media are thus not neutral disseminators of information because the nature of the construction and interpretation processes entail bias and social influence.

Semiotics, the science of signs and how meanings are socially produced from the structural relations in sign systems, has contributed greatly to media literacy. Roland Barthes explains that semiotics aims to challenge the naturalness of a message, the "what-goes-with-out-saying" (1998, p. 11). Masterman (1994) asserts that the foundation of media education is the principle of non-transparency. Media do not present reality like transparent windows or simple reflections of the world because media messages are created, shaped, and positioned through a construction process. This construction involves many decisions about what to include or exclude and how to represent reality. Masterman explains non-transparency with a pun: "the media do not present reality, they re-present it" (1994, p. 33). Giroux writes, "What appears as 'natural' must be demystified and revealed as a historical production both in its content, with its unrealized claims or distorting messages, and in the elements that structure its form" (1997, pp. 79–80). Exposing the choices involved in the construction process is an important starting point for critical inquiry because it disrupts the myth that media can be neutral conveyors of information.

Each core concept has a key question attached to it as a way for teachers to introduce abstract ideas through an inquiry process. The *Key Question* used with this concept (Who created this message?) encourages students to question authorship as a step toward understanding that all messages are created by somebody, often many people. Media production offers the potential to demonstrate this concept through hands-on work; however, the principle of non-transparency needs to be made obvious. Too often media production focuses exclusively on production skills and the final product at the expense of critical analysis. Students at the Leo Politi Elementary School were encouraged to create media with each thematic unit as a vehicle to analyze *how* the construction process represents reality. Using production to teach analysis is an approach that Australian media educator Carmen Luke suggests parents use with children as young as 3 years of age. Involving children in the production process of making home movies, according to Luke, can "enhance their understanding of the constructed aspect of TV. This is the first step in demystifying TV by enabling them literally to see and become aware of how TV reality is created by people and technology" (1990, p. 93).

Many SMARTArt teachers had their students take pictures of each other from different camera angles. When the tallest student in class was photographed from a high camera angle and the shortest was seen from a low camera angle, the students concretely experienced the manipulation of the camera to portray people differently. Students explored the same ideas when they manipulated light and composition while taking pictures (see Share, 2005, lesson plans 2A and 2B). Reflection and analysis are important components in the pedagogical approach necessary to drive a critical understanding that brings awareness of the core concepts of media literacy. During production activities, SMARTArt teachers guided their students to question other media representations that use similar techniques to those they were using to create their media.[9] Comparisons to mainstream media texts such as newspapers, magazines, and TV programs are helpful to dissolve the myth of transparency and better prepare students to deconstruct media messages.

Core Concept #2: Codes and Conventions

Media Messages Are Constructed Using a Creative Language with Its Own Rules

The second core concept also relies heavily on semiotics to give concreteness to analysis about *how* signs and symbols function. From the study of semiotics, media literacy practitioners analyze the existence of dual meanings of signs: *denotation* (the more literal reference to content) and *connotation* (the more associative, subjective significations of a message based on ideological and cultural codes) (Hall, 1980). When connotation and denotation become one and the same, the representation appears natural, making the historical and social construction invisible (Fiske, 1990, p. 87). Therefore, the goal of the second concept is to help students distinguish between connotation and denotation. With younger students the terms are simplified into separating what they *see* or *hear* from what they *think* or *feel*. Creating media can be a powerful vehicle for guiding students to explore these ideas and learn how different codes and conventions function.

SMARTArt students used the visual and performing arts to integrate media literacy with different subject areas, and in so doing, they learned the different languages intrinsic to each art form. Using visual arts, students applied the elements of design to posters they created that reflected their concerns from a social studies unit on urban wildlife. Through theater activities, a third grade class wrote and performed a story about the differences between the fantasy and real life of a cartoon hero. Students used dance to communicate with movements and express feelings. Music lessons helped students explore the camouflaged role sounds play in influencing emotions while viewing images (see Share, 2005, lesson plan 2D). Classes watched a video several times of chimpanzees swinging through trees. During each viewing, different music accompanied the images and offered opportunities to experience the different effects music can have on images. Later, students applied these experiences when they created their own soundtracks to accompany animation they had drawn.

Although the goal of the first concept is simply an awareness of the constructed nature of all media, this second concept focuses the exploration onto *how* the message is constructed. There is much overlap in teaching and learning media literacy since communication is a complex and organic process that does not naturally divide into distinct areas. The photography exercises from the first concept, the art lessons mentioned above, and the activities listed below all offer many opportunities to teach multiple concepts at the same time.

Core Concept #3: Audience

Different People Experience the Same Media Message Differently

The third core concept evolves from work at the Centre for Contemporary Cultural Studies at the University of Birmingham in England, where the notion of an active audience challenged previous theories that viewed receivers of media as passive recipients and often victims. This is a major advance for understanding literacy as Ien Ang explains, "Textual meanings do not reside in the texts themselves: a certain text can come to mean different things depending on the interdiscursive context in which viewers interpret it" (2002, p. 180). The notion that audiences are neither powerless nor omnipotent when it comes to reading media contributes greatly to the potential for media literacy to empower audiences in the process of negotiating meanings. "While audiences are clearly not passive and are able to pick and choose, it is simultaneously true that there are certain 'received' messages that are rarely mediated by the will of the audience," writes bell hooks (1996, p. 3). Empowering the audience through critical thinking inquiry is essential for students to challenge the power of media to create preferred readings. British audience theory views the moment of reception as a contested terrain of cultural struggle where critical thinking skills offer potential for the audience to negotiate different readings and openly struggle with dominant discourses.

The ability for students to see how different people can interpret the same message differently is also important for multicultural education since understanding differences means more than merely tolerating one another. Multicultural education for a pluralistic democracy depends on a citizenry that embraces multiple perspectives as a natural consequence of different experiences, histories, and cultures constructed within structures of dominance and subordination. Understanding different ways of seeing is essential to understanding the politics of representation. John Berger writes, "The way we see things is affected by what we know or what we believe" (1977, p. 8).

An activity that some SMARTArt teachers used to explore this concept involved dividing the class into separate advertising agencies and assigning different target audiences to each team. Students were required to design an advertising campaign to sell a product to their assigned audience (see Share, 2005, lesson plan 3D). A fifth grade class conducted this activity using the plants from a science lesson and created posters to present as commercials for five different audiences. Their target audiences were preschoolers like their younger siblings, kids just like themselves, their grandparents, teenage girls, and wealthy white middle-aged males. The students were highly motivated and produced very different advertisements that as authentic assessment helped demonstrate their understanding about how different people experience media messages differently.

Core Concept #4: Content and Message

Media Have Embedded Values and Points of View

The fourth concept involves the politics of representation in which the form and content of media messages are interrogated in order to question ideology, bias, and the connotations explicit and implicit in the representation. Cultural studies, feminist theory, and critical pedagogy offer arsenals of research for this line of inquiry to question media representations of race, class, gender, sexuality, and the like. Beyond simply locating the bias in media, this concept helps students recognize the subjective nature of all communication.

Through questioning and creating, SMARTArt students searched for the underlying messages in advertising as well as the more latent values communicated in currency and maps (see Share, 2005, lesson plans 1E and 3B). A third grade teacher had her students create two versions of a school newspaper.[10] Students photographed school staff using production techniques to create very different images of the same people. They then interviewed the staff members for the first publication that presented the positive perspective of the school with flattering photographs. The second publication consisted of scary photographs and fictional writing about the same staff members published as humor. In addition to providing meaningful learning for the students, these publications also offered authentic assessment to demonstrate student comprehension of the concept that values are embedded in media. While creating these publications, students analyzed representations of race and gender in their city newspaper. Their results informed their production activities and led them to reconsider issues of gender imbalance that they had overlooked in their own work.

Core Concept #5: Motivation and Political Economy

Media Are Organized to Gain Profit and/or Power

The final concept encourages students to consider the question of *why* the message was sent and *where* it came from. Too often students believe the role of media is simply to entertain or inform, with little knowledge of the economic structure that supports it. Where once there were many media outlets in every city competing for viewers and readers, a few years ago there were fewer than 10 transnational corporations dominating the global media market. In the latest edition of Ben Bagdikian's *The New Media Monopoly* (2004), Bagdikian states that there are just five corporations that dominate the U.S. media market. He writes:

> Five global-dimension firms, operating with many of the characteristics of a cartel, own most of the newspapers, magazines, book publishers, motion picture studios, and radio and television stations in the United States . . . These five conglomerates are Time Warner, by 2003 the largest media firm in the world; The Walt Disney Company; Murdoch's News Corporation, based in Australia; Viacom; and Bertelsmann, based in Germany. (p. 3)

The consolidation of ownership of the mass media has given control of the public airwaves to a few multinational oligopolies to determine who and what is represented and how. This concentration of ownership threatens the independence and diversity of information and creates the possibility for the global colonization of culture and knowledge (McChesney, 2004). Robert McChesney insists that the consolidated ownership of the media giants is highly undemocratic, fundamentally noncompetitive, and "more closely resembles a cartel than it does the competitive marketplace found in economics textbooks" (1999, p. 13).

Bringing ideas of media ownership to elementary school students can be addressed by instruction that asks *Key Question* #5: Why was this message sent? SMARTArt students deconstructed and created advertising to convince other people about issues they were studying in language arts, science, or social studies. Lower grade teachers had their students begin by separating advertisements from editorial content and then products from brands (see Share, 2005, lesson plan 2E). Older students analyzed techniques of persuasion, kept track of who was renting their eyeballs, and created posters that spoofed and made fun of advertising fallacies. Though different activities are more appropriate for different developmental levels, most students from kindergarten on up have the cognitive ability to understand that the primary goal of advertising is to sell. Since advertising is the motor that runs the mass media, it is important that students understand the economic motivation behind commercial media. When students are aware of who created a media artifact, they can better inquire into why it was created and in turn be better prepared to recognize systemic biases and distortions.

Critical Pedagogy and Critical Theory

The core concepts of media literacy are most relevant to progressive and transformative education when taught through a democratic approach with critical pedagogy that follows ideas of progressive educators like John Dewey and Paulo Freire. Without a critical frame, the core concepts can become tools for instrumental progressivism (Robins & Webster, 2001) and lose their radical potential (Ferguson, 2000). As ideas about media education are beginning to take hold across the U.S., it is imperative that critical pedagogy be a central component.

Antonia Darder, Marta Baltodano, and Rodolfo Torres write about the history of critical pedagogy and pay homage to John Dewey as having "had a significant influence on progressive educators concerned with advancing democratic ideals in education" (2003, p. 3). Dewey appreciated the power of the environment and considered understanding and connecting with the environment essential to education. He writes, "the environment consists of those conditions that promote or hinder, stimulate or inhibit, the *characteristic* activities of a living being" (1916/1997, p. 11). It is through acting upon the environment that Dewey asserts life becomes "a self-renewing process" (p. 2). For most students in the U.S. today, a major part of their environment is media, and critical media literacy provides a direct path to act upon that environment.

This lifelong process of learning is based on a positive concept of growth as perpetual evolution. Dewey states, "The primary condition of growth is immaturity . . . the prefix 'im' of the word immaturity means something positive, not a mere void or lack" (p. 41). By viewing children as immature, Dewey posits children as different than animals since they have the capacity to grow, change, and evolve. He also sees education as an essential part of the evolutionary process necessary for social reproduction and human survival. Dewey does not view the goal of education as helping humanity to merely endure and reproduce the status quo; his vision for education aims mankind in the direction of prevailing and transforming society into a socially just democracy.

Education for Dewey is about citizenship and democracy, not about specialized job training that benefits business over individuals and perpetuates social inequality. He states, "Education would then become an instrument of perpetuating unchanged the existing industrial order of society, instead of operating as a means of its transformation" (p. 316). This is a major concern today as neoliberalism, school vouchers, and business partnerships with educational institutions move to privatize the public sphere, including education. Dewey writes, "A democracy is more than a form of government; it is primarily a mode of associated living, of conjoint communicated experience" (p. 87). He stresses the need for public education to be

> a means of transformation. The desired transformation is not difficult to define in a formal way. It signifies a society in which every person shall be occupied in something which makes the lives of others better worth living, and which accordingly makes the ties which bind persons together more perceptible—which breaks down the barriers of distance between them. (p. 316)

Transformative education requires a critical pedagogy of solidarity in which empathy and compassion help students understand the ways people are interconnected through systems of dominance and subordination.

Dewey's progressive goals of democracy become practical through his pragmatic approach to teaching based upon experience. He insists, "Every experience is a moving force. Its value can be judged only on the ground of what it moves toward and into" (1938/1963, p. 38). Dewey envisions progressive education as a continual spiral where the teacher creates curiosity through structuring experiences for students to engage, explore, and experiment. As they actively challenge new experiences, their inquiry continues to spiral out into more questions and connections with more experiences. He explains, "Unless a given experience leads out into a field previously unfamiliar no problems arise, while problems are the stimulus to thinking. That the conditions found in present experience should be used as sources of problems is a characteristic which differentiates education based upon experience from traditional education" (p. 79).

Dewey makes a distinction between his progressive education and traditional education (similar to Freire's description of *banking education*) that is concerned with social conformity and transmission of facts. In line with his goals of democracy, Dewey places great emphasis on the need for active learning, experimentation, and problem solving. He asserts that education will be interesting to students when they perceive a meaningful connection between themselves and the material. Dewey's pragmatic approach connects theory with practice and requires students to similarly connect reflection with action. He writes, "Numbers are not objects of study just because they are numbers already constituting a branch of learning called mathematics, but because they represent qualities and relations of the world in which our action goes on, because they are factors upon which the accomplishments of our purposes depends" (1916/1997, p. 134).

Dewey offers a wealth of advice about education that is desperately missing from today's theory and practice. For media literacy to be transformative, it must be taught through a critical pedagogy based primarily on Dewey's progressive education. He writes,

> Knowledge is humanistic in quality not because it is about human products in the past, but because of what it does in liberating human intelligence and human sympathy. Any subject matter which accomplishes this result is humane, and any subject matter which does not accomplish it is not even educational. (1916/1997, p. 230)

Through combining media production with critical analysis, critical media literacy holds potential to create libratory pedagogy.

The other key figure in the development of progressive education and critical pedagogy is Brazilian educator Paulo Freire. Darder et al. write, "Freire is considered by many to be the most influential educational philosopher in the development of critical pedagogical thought and practice" (2003, p. 5). Both Dewey and Freire are critical of the established educational systems, proponents of progressive social change, and believers in the need to unite theory with practice. However, Dewey's liberal reform is less radical than Freire's revolutionary pedagogy based on liberation from oppression. The two men see humans as being in the process of evolving and education as an important tool to assist people in becoming more humane and complete. While Dewey opposes dualism, Freire's dialectical perspective defines freedom as the opposite of oppression. Freire writes, "Concern for humanization leads at once to the recognition of dehumanization, not only as an ontological possibility but as an historical reality" (1970, p. 27).

Freire's critical pedagogy is radically political in its call for *conscientização*, a revolutionary critical consciousness that involves perception as well as action against oppression. He proposes a *problem-posing pedagogy* as a liberating alternative to the dehumanizing *banking education* that can still be found today in most schools around the world. Freire describes banking education as an alienating system that deposits fragments of information into passive students like money into a bank. He explains that the real teaching accomplished by banking education is a hidden curriculum that indoctrinates and pacifies, "for the more the oppressed can be led to adapt to that situation, the more easily they can be dominated" (p. 60).

The problem-posing alternative that Freire preaches requires dialogical communication between students and teachers where both are learning and teaching each other. He states, "one must seek to live *with* others in solidarity. One cannot impose oneself, nor even merely co-exist with one's students. Solidarity requires true communication" (p. 63). This is a revolutionary act that necessitates praxis, critical reflection together with action to transform society. Freire writes, "In dialectical thought, world and action are intimately interdependent" (p. 38).

For Freire, liberation pedagogy involves the process of moving from being an object of history to becoming a critically aware *subject* of one's own situation. The oppressed often fail to recognize their own oppression when they believe the myths of the oppressor and blame themselves. Freire writes, as the oppressed becomes a subject, "as he breaks his 'adhesion' and objectifies the reality from which he starts to emerge, he begins to integrate himself as a Subject (an *I*) confronting an object (reality). At this moment, sundering the false unity of his divided self, he becomes a true individual" (p. 174).

This pedagogy cannot be authoritative; it requires a humanist, revolutionary educator to be a partner in the struggle for liberation. Freire explains that teachers and students "are both Subjects, not only in the task of unveiling that reality, and thereby coming to know it critically, but in the task of re-creating that knowledge. As they attain this knowledge of reality through common reflection and action, they discover themselves as its permanent re-creators" (p. 56). This is an empowering pedagogy that offers agency and hope for both students and teachers, especially when new media technologies become tools for creating alternative messages.

An aspect of Freire's philosophy that can be quite useful for media literacy is his description of antidialogical mythicizing. He explains that in order for the dominant minority to oppress the majority, they need to increase the alienation and passivity of the oppressed. This is achieved through the hegemonic myths that are taught in schools, repeated in the media, and naturalized through the dominant society's worldview. Freire writes that the oppressive myths "are presented to them by well-organized propaganda and slogans, via the mass 'communications' media—as if such alienation constituted real communication" (p. 136). This understanding of the role media play in maintaining hegemony and oppression led Freire to suggest that problem-posing education needs to present these myths to students as problems to be unveiled through dialogue. He writes, "It is not the media themselves which I criticize, but the way they are used" (p. 136). Critical media literacy can help students deconstruct the myths and take action to create counterhegemonic media whereby students become the subjects and name their world. Through denaturalizing media representations, students can expose the workings of ideology. However, it is not enough to just identify sexist, racist, classist, or homophobic messages or their origins; students should be encouraged to question how these oppressive ideologies are sustained and create alternative messages that expose and challenge the ideological structures.

Critical media literacy is more difficult to teach than most apolitical approaches to media education because of the complexity and invisibility of how ideology functions. Robert Ferguson writes, "'Ideology' is not directly visible, but can only be experienced and/or comprehended. What is visible is a range of social and representational manifestations which are rooted in relationships of power and subordination" (1998, p. 43). Through the process of *naturalizing* power relations, ideology removes from view their social and historical construction. What one does not see, one rarely questions. Therefore, progressive educators should guide students to ask critical questions that will help reveal the structures, history, and social contexts that are too often obscured from view by ideological hegemony.

Ferguson asserts, "the relationship of consciousness to ideology is not psychological or moralistic in character, but 'structural and epistemological.' This means that it has to do with the ways in which knowledge and understanding are constructed and defended" (1998, p. 44). He suggests that humans make meaning by accessing internalized sets of reference points that he calls our *discursive reserve*. Ferguson writes, "The values, judgements and opinions upon which we draw are always negotiated in relation to a discursive reserve, which in turn is socially acquired and sustained" (2004, p. 11). He suggests that a discursive reserve is usually invoked through Herbert Paul Grice's notion of *implicature*, the way one fills in the blanks of that which is unsaid yet inferred. Many institutions in society construct discourses, not the least being the media, whose dominant presence and ubiquitous transmedia intertextuality stimulate and feed copious discursive reserves on a global scale (Kinder, 1991).

Ideology functions through the implicatures that occur as people tap into their discursive reserves to determine who and what is "normal" as compared to all else that becomes the "other." The ideological discourse of "normality" is constructed through "othering" all that is not the "norm." Ferguson states, "The invocation of normality and the establishment of culturally and politically acceptable behavioural patterns often form the keystone for ideological arguments made at the expense of individuals, groups, or nations deemed to be 'other'" (p. 154). Stuart Hall writes, "Ideologies tend to disappear from view into the taken-for-granted 'naturalised' world of common sense. Since (like gender) race appears to be 'given' by Nature, racism is one of the most profoundly 'naturalised' of existing ideologies" (2003, p. 90).

Ferguson suggests that one reason race is such an important issue for media educators is "[b]ecause most of the information about 'others' and 'race' is available only through the mass media, the international or global dimension of representing 'race' is even more problematic than that which is concerned with local or regional affairs. Images of issues of 'race' are likely to be multiple, fragmented and transitory" (1998, p. 253). Multicultural educator James Banks (2000) asserts, "The representations of people and groups in the media is a cogent factor that influences children's perceptions, attitudes, and values" (p. xiii). Carlos Cortés (2000) writes, "The enveloping media multicultural curriculum guarantees that school educators do not have the power to decide *if* multicultural education will occur. It will . . . through the media, even if not in schools" (p. xvi). Cortés is a leader in promoting a brand of media literacy that prioritizes multiculturalism to help students distinguish between generalizations and stereotypes. He writes that the mass media multicultural curriculum does not *cause* racism but it does *contribute* "significantly to the corpus of American thinking, feeling, and acting in the realm of diversity" (p. 69). He suggests that the power of media to influence children's notions of "the other" comes from the "frequency and variety" of representations (p. 154). According to Ferguson, the most common representations of race tend to concentrate on individual figures more than social formations, thereby softening the "systematic processes of historical racism" (1998, p. 218). Ferguson suggests that a historic perspective is important because it helps to see race not as natural or arbitrary, but rather as an ideological construction.

Patricia Hill Collins (2000) asserts, "an increasingly important dimension of why hegemonic ideologies concerning race, class, gender, sexuality, and nation remain so deeply entrenched lies, in part, in the growing sophistication of mass media in regulating intersecting oppressions" (p. 284). She states that dominant representations of black women in the media are controlling images that objectify and subordinate. Collins writes, "Portraying African-American women as stereotypical mammies, matriarchs, welfare recipients, and hot mommas helps justify U.S. Black women's oppression" (p. 69). Even though the specific images and stereotypes may change, Collins insists that "the overall ideology of domination itself seems to be an enduring feature of intersecting oppressions" (p. 88).

From studying the ideological structures of patriarchy, many feminist theorists like Collins developed feminist standpoint epistemologies that can be useful for critical media literacy. The construction of hegemony veils and denies alternative epistemologies, thereby reinforcing the dominant ideology as the only correct way of seeing and understanding. These ruling ideas are essential for the maintenance of the social hierarchies that privilege some and oppress others. Therefore, in order to create a more egalitarian society, we must break hegemonic control of patriarchy, white supremacy, imperialism, classism, homophobia, and other oppressive ideologies by exposing the structures of privilege and oppression. This change requires more than simply revealing new information; it requires new ways of thinking and understanding. Collins writes, "Alternative knowledge claims in and of themselves are rarely threatening to conventional knowledge" (2000, p. 270) because they can easily be ignored, discredited, or co-opted. However, alternative epistemologies are truly dangerous to hegemony because they not only challenge existing ideas, but they also challenge the *process* of deciding what counts as truth. Collins states, "If the epistemology used to evaluate knowledge comes into question, then all prior knowledge claims validated under the dominant model become suspect. Alternative epistemologies challenge all certified knowledge and open up the question of whether what has been taken to be true can stand the test of alternative ways of validating truth" (2000, p. 271).

Feminist standpoint epistemologies offer a methodology to empower the marginalized and a process for deconstructing society's dominant myths that hide the links between knowledge and power. This methodology is a guide for political, intellectual, and collective struggle that studies up from subordinate positions to reveal structures of oppression, the functioning of hegemony, and alternative epistemologies. Sandra Harding writes,

> Standpoint theories argue for "starting off thought" from the lives of marginalized peoples; beginning in those determinate, objective locations in any social order will generate illuminating critical questions that do not arise in thought that begins from dominant group lives. (2004, p. 128)

Marginalized voices offer the potential to access experiences and insight that are missing from dominant discourse, thereby strengthening objectivity. Since people in oppressed situations live the effects of oppression, they have the potential to see it and understand it much clearer than most oppressors. Uma Narayan states:

> it is *easier* and *more likely* for the oppressed to have critical insights into the conditions of their own oppression than it is for those who live outside these structures. Those who actually *live* the oppressions of class, race, or gender have faced the issues that

such oppressions generate in a variety of different situations. The insights and emotional responses engendered by these situations are a legacy with which they confront any new issue or situation. (2004, p. 220)

Collins suggests that marginalized people hold a unique position in society as outsiders within, and this location offers them greater ability to see anomalies of omission and distortion in the "taken-for-granted assumptions" of the normalized hegemony. She explains, "where white males may take it as perfectly normal to generalize findings from studies of white males to other groups, Black women are more likely to see such a practice as problematic, as an anomaly" (p. 119). The omission of observations and facts is more obvious to the people who see themselves overlooked or excluded. When this information is not missing, it is often distorted and marginalized. Subordinate positions also offer potential to spot anomalies of misrepresentation. Collins writes,

while Black women have and are themselves mothers they encounter distorted versions of themselves and their mothers under the mantle of the Black matriarchy thesis . . . The response to these perceived distortions has been one of redefining distorted images—for example, debunking the Sapphire and Mammy myths. (2004, p. 120)

While people who experience oppression have greater potential for understanding the structures of oppression, critical consciousness is not automatic. Nancy Hartsock writes,

the vision available to the oppressed group must be struggled for and represents an achievement which requires both science to see beneath the surface of the social relations in which all are forced to participate, and the education which can only grow from struggle to change those relations. (1997, p. 153)

Stressing the importance of the struggle to come to consciousness, Antonia Darder writes:

The consequence is that very often people of color whose bicultural voices and experiences have been systematically silenced and negated are not necessarily conscious of the manner in which racism and classism have influenced their individual development, nor how they have functioned to distort perceptions of their cultural group within an Anglocentric world. Therefore the fact that a person is bicultural does not guarantee that she or he occupies a position of resistance to such domination. (1997, p. 345)

Standpoint theories are not simply points of view from oppressed people. Harding insists, "It cannot be overemphasized that the epistemic privilege oppressed groups possess is by no means automatic. The 'moment of critical insight' is one that comes only through political struggle, for it is blocked and its understandings obscured by the dominant, hegemonous ideologies and the practices that they make appear normal and even natural" (2004, p. 9). Critical insight requires collective, intellectual, and political work to unveil the structures of oppression.

Subordinate positions do not automatically impart critical consciousness; however, they do offer tremendous potential. bell hooks suggests, "understanding marginality as position and place of resistance is crucial for oppressed, exploited, colonized people" (2004, p. 157). hooks writes, "I make a definite distinction between that marginality which is imposed by the oppressive structures and that marginality one chooses as site of resistance—as location of radical openness and possibility" (2004, p. 159). Standpoint epistemologies that look at all forms of oppression as starting points offer important strategies for beginning critical media literacy projects. When problem-posing education begins from the perspective of subordinate groups, the problems posed will more likely address issues of power and oppression. As a beginning point for critical media literacy inquiry, standpoint epistemologies illuminate hegemonic structures in media representations.

The power to dominate through the objectification of the "Other" is an essential structural component of oppression. Therefore, the ability to disrupt the objectifying of marginalized people and challenge the system by empowering the oppressed to become politicized subjects is extremely important. Collins writes, "defining and valuing one's consciousness of one's own self-defined standpoint in the face of images that foster a self-definition as the objectified 'other' is an important way of resisting the dehumanization essential to systems of domination" (2004, p. 108). She states, "When Black women define themselves, they clearly reject the taken-for-granted assumptions that those in positions granting them the authority to describe and analyze reality are entitled to do so ... the act of insisting on Black female self-definition validates Black women's power as human subjects" (2004, pp. 106–107). Monique Wittig writes:

> When we discover that women are the objects of oppression and appropriation, at the very moment that we become able to perceive this, we become subjects in the sense of cognitive subjects, through an operation of abstraction. Consciousness of oppression is not only a reaction to (fight against) oppression. It is also the whole conceptual reevaluation of the social world, its whole reorganization with new concepts, from the point of view of oppression. (1997, p. 225)

Moving from being an object to becoming a subject can be politically and personally liberating, as Freire asserts. Coming to voice can be a liberating act of resistance for oppressed and exploited people. hooks states, "We come to this space through suffering and pain, through struggle. We know struggle to be that which pleasures, delights, and fulfills desire. We are transformed, individually, collectively, as we make radical creative space which affirms and sustains our subjectivity, which gives us a new location from which to articulate our sense of the world" (2004, p. 159).

Standpoint epistemologies offer a methodology for beginning one's study of oppression from the bottom up as a way of bringing alternative epistemological frameworks into the political struggle of education and social change for women, minorities, the poor, or any people who experience oppression. The process of studying up is essential for exposing hegemonic blind spots and reversing typical top-down research and media that objectify subjects as they represent them. Critical pedagogy also studies up, as marginalized students become the subjects of their learning through critical inquiry and social action. Critical media literacy that combines critical pedagogy with standpoint epistemologies can offer an approach to help marginalized students see the structures of oppression, analyze the role of hegemony in shrouding those structures, and find agency in the act of becoming subjects who can express their voices to challenge racism, sexism, classism, and all forms of oppression.

Creating alternative media and coming to voice is important for people who have seldom been allowed to speak for themselves, but without critical analysis, it is not enough. Critical analysis that explores and exposes the structures of oppression is essential because merely coming to voice is something any marginalized racist or sexist group of people can also claim. Spaces must be opened up and opportunities created so that people in subaltern positions have the opportunity to collectively struggle against oppression to voice their concerns and create their own alternative representations. By changing the starting point of inquiry, from top down to bottom up, the potential is greater for everyone to build a critical consciousness that can empathize with the oppressed and pierce through the hegemony to see the institutions and systems that dominate.

Through group discussions, critical analysis, and political struggle, classrooms can be transformed into spaces of libratory pedagogy and not simply social reproduction. Marginalized voices and perspectives offer great potential to challenge dominant discourse by exposing the myth that information and knowledge can be objective and separate from power. Michel Foucault writes "that there is no power relation without the correlative constitution of a field of knowledge, nor any knowledge that does not presuppose and constitute at the same time power relations" (1995, p. 27). Since people with desires, fears, and prejudices construct ideas within social and historical contexts, there is no information or knowledge that is ever objective or neutral. Harding explains, "The more value-neutral a conceptual framework appears, the more likely it is to advance the hegemonous interests of dominant groups, and less likely it is to be able to detect important actualities of social relations" (2004, p. 6). A strategy for counteracting hegemony is exposing its construction and unveiling the biases inherent in all communication.

Freire's *problem-posing* education that encourages students to collectively engage with problems and then wrestle with solving them can fit well with standpoint theory. He writes, "cooperation leads dialogical Subjects to focus their attention on the reality which mediates them and which—posed as a problem—challenges them. The response to that challenge is the action of dialogical Subjects upon reality in order to transform it" (1970, p. 168). Jane Flax suggests that with successful feminism, "'reality' will appear even more unstable, complex, and disorderly than it does now" (1997, p. 178). It is through problematizing reality that knowledge and stories from marginalized positions can have much greater potential to demystify hegemony and offer alternative epistemologies. When aiming for social transformation, students must begin inquiry from marginal positions and then study up as part of the process of collective political struggle. While this may sound too radical for public education, it is actually right in line with the basic principles of democracy and the U.S. Bill of Rights. Democracy and liberty require a type of literacy that goes far beyond the mere ability to read and write. Henry Giroux states, "To be literate is *not* to be free, it is to be present and active in the struggle for reclaiming one's voice, history, and future" (1987, p. 11).

Standpoint epistemologies can lead critical pedagogues in the political struggle for social justice. Educators should begin the inquiry process by listening to subordinate voices and then guide their students in collective struggle for understanding the systems and epistemologies that perpetuate hegemony. Through this struggle, critical pedagogy can help students to study up to uncover the systems that make racist, sexist, and other oppressive ideas appear normal. As students become subjects of their own representations, they become agents of change who can take action to rewrite and correct the omissions and distortions of oppressive ideologies. They can challenge the structures and institutions that maintain hierarchal privileges for the few and subordination for the majority. The power of hegemony to hide itself under commonsense assumptions diminishes in the light of alternative epistemologies and politically empowered subjects. Media literacy's principle of non-transparency embraces this notion of hegemony that when media are considered transparent windows on the world, they obtain hegemonic powers. Therefore, non-transparency means exposing core concept #1, "all media messages are constructed," because many choices have been made that could have been made differently and can be changed once people recognize the structures of hegemony.

If students learn to deconstruct and construct media with a critical media literacy framework and through a standpoint methodology, they are far more likely to recognize hegemonic myths, understand the oppression they cause, and want to act in solidarity with those struggling for their rights. Perhaps a deeper understanding of the true functioning of the world requires changing core concept #1 to read, all media messages are *co-constructed*. Harding uses the term *co-constructivism* "to emphasize how systematic knowledge-seeking is always just one element in any culture, society, or social formation in its local environment, shifting and transforming other elements—education systems, legal systems, economic relations, religious beliefs and practices, state projects (such as war-making), gender relations—as it, in turn, is transformed by them" (1998, p. 4). This description of co-constructivism can be useful to demythologize the social construction process and at the same time expose the interconnectedness of people, ideas, and society. Harding writes, "We can retain the best of both realist and constructivist understandings of the relations between our social worlds, our representations, and the realities our representations are intended to represent by thinking of co-evolving, or co-constructing, cultures and their knowledge projects" (1998, p. 20).

Understanding these interconnections and interdependence is necessary, according to Robert Ferguson, to create *critical solidarity* (2001). Ferguson suggests that our relationships with media are not autonomous, but rather they depend on taking positions related to social contexts. Since we are always taking sides, Ferguson calls for critical solidarity as "a means by which we acknowledge the social dimensions of our thinking and analysis. It is also a means through which we may develop our skills of analysis and relative autonomy" (2001, p. 42). Critical solidarity means teaching students to interpret information and communication within humanistic, social, historical, political, and economic contexts for them to understand the interrelationships and consequences of their actions and lifestyles. It also means joining in solidarity with the disempowered in a collective struggle for a more just world.

Conclusion

Media education is a new concept in the U.S., and already aspects of it can be found in almost all of the 50 state educational frameworks.[11] At this point, when ideas about media education are beginning to take hold across the continent, it is imperative that critical pedagogy and standpoint theory be central components. This is a radical break from traditional education as standpoint epistemologies link struggles against oppression with media representations. Critical pedagogy should be built upon a solid foundation that applies ideas from John Dewey's experiential education and Paulo Freire's problem-posing pedagogy. These educational theories require learning to begin with what students already know, build on their experiences, confront the problems they experience in their daily lives, and express their ideas and concerns to audiences beyond the classroom. Student-centered education should spiral out into new areas of learning as students explore and search for meanings. When the goal of critical solidarity guides media education, standpoint theory provides a model for inquiry that exposes hegemony and the structures of power in society. Freire insists that students must be involved in unveiling and demythologizing reality (1970).

CHAPTER THREE

Critical Media Literacy Is Not an Option

Overview of Media Education in the U.S. and Abroad

For most of the 55 million students in kindergarten through high school in the U.S., critical media literacy is not an option because it is not available; it is not even on the radar. Unlike educators in Canada, Great Britain, and Australia, many in the U.S. are not informed enough about media literacy to even consider it. Yet, in today's multimedia world, it is insufficient to teach literacy that only addresses traditional concepts of print while ignoring the other major ways we receive, process, and create images and information. Critical media literacy is an educational response that expands the notion of literacy to include different forms of mass communication, popular culture, and new technologies as well as deepens the potential of literacy education to critically analyze relationships between media and audiences, information and power. Along with this critical analysis, alternative media production empowers students to create their own messages that can challenge ideological media texts and narratives. In the contemporary era of standardized high-stakes testing and corporate solicitations in public education, the question we must ask is not *whether* critical media literacy should be taught, but instead, *how* it should be taught.

In various areas across the U.S., dozens of organizations and individuals are teaching critical thinking skills about media to students, teachers, community members, inmates, health care professionals, and others. The U.S. has two national media literacy membership organizations that hold national conferences every 2 years, support a variety of media literacy activities, and claim about 400 members each. There are also numerous blogs and cybergroups based in the U.S. dedicated to media literacy.[1]

The larger of the two organizations, the National Association for Media Literacy Education (NAMLE) founded in 2001 as the Alliance for a Media Literate America (AMLA), is an umbrella organization of many independent media literacy organizations. NAMLE attempts to unite media literacy organizations as well as commercial media makers, whereas the other national media literacy organization takes an ardent position against any type of commercial collaboration or sponsorship. Although the two groups have similar goals, their philosophical differences reflect a fissure in media education in the U.S.

Founded in 2002, Action Coalition for Media Education (ACME) rejects any ties to corporate media and supports an activist position in relation to media regulation and ownership. At the founding of ACME, Sut Jhally (2002), founder and executive director of the Media Education Foundation, described the division within the media literacy movement in the U.S. as a difference in starting points. He suggests that many begin their analysis stressing the *literacy* aspect of messages, whereas the correct starting point should instead stress the context of the message. Jhally's institutional analysis reflects the ACME focus on the *media* part of media literacy. However, Faith Rogow (2004), former president of AMLA, asserts that stressing media over literacy is pedagogically "fatally flawed" (p. 30). She suggests that by placing the primary focus on literacy, media literacy will become more of an academic field than a social movement. This division reveals key differences between NAMLE's more liberal educational approach and ACME's more radical advocacy position.

Although many media educators are members of both organizations, personal differences between some of the leaders have hindered collaboration. Media education in the U.S. is having more success on smaller levels by hardworking individuals and small organizations. One example of success can be seen in the unconnected work by people across the country to advance media literacy concepts into state standards.

Today, most of the 50 states in the U.S. make some mention of media education in their educational standards (Kubey & Baker, 1999). Frank Baker maintains an online listing of media literacy standards in different states that identify under which subject matter media education can be found in each state's standards (http://www.frankwbaker.com/state_lit.htm).[2] For example, in California, the State Department of Education lists the category "Analysis and Evaluation of Oral and Media Communications" as part of Language Arts for third through twelfth grades. In Texas, media education is included in the state standards under the heading of "Viewing and Representing" within Language Arts Standards from fourth grade on. The closest equivalent the U.S. has to national educational standards can be found at the Mid-continent Research for Education and Learning (McREL) organization. This private nonprofit organization is a leader in educational standards for many state departments of education. Online they list "Viewing" (uses viewing skills and strategies to understand and interpret visual media) and "Media" (understands the characteristics and components of the media) as two of the five components of Language Arts.[3] Although media education is now expected to be taught as it is listed in all the state standards, unfortunately little has been done to train teachers, provide resources, or create curriculum.

Teacher training programs that specifically focus on media education in the U.S. are few and far between. Only a few organizations offer trainings like the annual weeklong New Mexico Media Literacy Project's *Catalyst Institute* or Project Look Sharp's *Media Literacy Summer Institute* in Ithaca, New York.

More recently, the Media Education Lab at Temple University began offering workshops for teachers in the Philadelphia area, and the University of Southern California's Annenberg Center began training teachers through their Institute for Multimedia Literacy. Scattered across the U.S. are universities and colleges offering a course or two in media education, usually dependent on a professor who happens to have a special interest in the subject (Silverblatt, Baker, Tyner & Stuhlman, 2002). Though many individuals and organizations are teaching media literacy, when compared with the immense size of the U.S. population, the percentage of media education actually happening is extremely small.

A few universities in the U.S. now offer comprehensive academic programs in media education. In North Carolina, the Appalachian State University offers a Master of Arts (MA) in Educational Media. This program was founded in 2000 by David Considine, who also runs an annual summer institute in media literacy at the university. Webster University in Missouri offers both a Bachelor of Arts (BA) and an MA with emphasis in media literacy.

It is more common to find a critical media class in a communication department than in a school of education. A big challenge for media literacy in the U.S. is thus to enter into teacher training programs and departments of education. Universities should be on the forefront of this movement. Bridges need to be built between communication departments or graduate schools of education that are doing progressive work in cultural studies and teacher education programs that are training new teachers. Too often these programs, sometimes housed in the same building, do not even know what the other is doing. If new teachers and new policy makers could be taught cultural studies theory and critical pedagogy practices, they could leave their ivy towers better prepared to work together to reframe literacy education. Carmen Luke warns, "unless educators take a lead in developing appropriate pedagogies for these new electronic media and forms of communication, corporate experts will be the ones to determine how people will learn, what they learn, and what constitutes literacy" (2000b, p. 71).

Unfortunately, most teacher training and staff development in the U.S. rarely mention media education or discuss media literacy concepts. This is still a brand new subject in the U.S. and has little awareness or support from many faculty and administrators. The current obsession with standardized high-stakes testing and the movement back to basics that has bumped critical thinking to the periphery, promoted by the Bush administration and conservative educators, makes the implementation of media education in the U.S. even more difficult. The precious little time in the classroom has become filled with test preparation and skill and drill. As the pendulum swings to the right, constructivist-based, child-centered programs such as "Whole Language" and "Core Literature" have been replaced by scripted phonics-based programs such as "Open Court Reading" and "Success for All." This positivist approach emphasizes memorization and testing skills over exploration and inquiry. It is movement away from Dewey's progressive advances and critical pedagogy and a return to what Freire called "banking education" (1970, p. 58). President George W. Bush's "No Child Left Behind Act" requires greater accountability in testing and promoting students and more severe consequences for failing to score on standardized tests. A harsher policy of grade-level retention has retarded the social development of students, who for numerous reasons score low on tests; the lack of funding by the Bush administration makes it difficult to provide the needed tutoring for failing students, thus greatly increasing the number of minority and poor students who cannot make it through high school.[4] These policies help reproduce a problematic deficit-thinking model of education where the students who fail are punished instead of helped.

The right-wing political agenda that has slashed educational budgets has been accompanied by reactionary legislation that has dismantled bilingual education and affirmative action. Jonathan Kozol (2005) describes the current state of public education in the U.S. as the restoration of apartheid, in which the wealthier, whiter suburban schools receive a quality of education far superior to the poorer inner-city schools that tend to teach predominantly African American and Hispanic youth. Accompanying this racial segregation is an anti-immigrant English-only agenda. During the 1990s in California, a series of state propositions attacked immigrants (Prop. 187), dismantled affirmative action (Prop. 209), and ended most of the state's bilingual education (Prop. 227).[5] Similar actions were also occurring in Texas and other states. These political attacks on immigrants continue and have led to student walkouts and massive demonstrations, such as the nearly 1 million people who protested in Los Angeles on March 25, 2006. The disproportional numbers of minorities being held back from promotion and dropping out of school reflect racial divisions and inequalities and the role of schools as sorting mechanisms for U.S. society.

Accompanying this conservative wave of positivism and discrimination is the corporate appropriation of progressive pedagogy under the label of instrumental progressivism. Uniting the business world with education is part of the co-opting of schools and the public sphere. Kevin Robins and Frank Webster (2001) explain that instrumental progressivism emphasizes competencies at the expense of content knowledge, increases monitoring and surveillance through excessive testing, and most importantly, disables critical thinking of its political potential. The morphing of corporate interests with educational institutions is less restrictive than outright censorship, yet more pernicious in its potential to set a corporate agenda for public education whereby students become commodities shaped to fit into the market economy as merely consumers and workers instead of citizens and active participants of a representational democracy.

This merging of corporate America with public education can clearly be seen in the Partnership for 21st Century Skills (http://www.21stcenturyskills.org/), a public–private organization founded in 2002 by the U.S. Department of Education, Microsoft Corporation, Apple Computer, Inc., and AOL Time Warner Foundation, to name a few. In a report released by this organization, media literacy is listed as a key learning skill. Although this partnership offers the possibility of wide exposure for media literacy, the danger of appropriation through instrumental progressivism is clear. The focus on workplace productivity and the absence of a social justice agenda demonstrate the influence of business interests.

Since the public schools reach the most students, they must be the front line of the battle for radical democracy, and yet there is much they can learn from some of the programs that are doing exemplary work in critical media literacy with students outside of the schoolroom.

Many community-based after-school programs like Educational Video

Center (EVC) in New York City and REACH LA in Los Angeles offer excellent examples of how media production can be taught as an essential component of critical media literacy. Both programs involve inner-city youth in video production activities in which the students explore their concerns and create their own alternative media to challenge the dominant representations. Founder and executive director of EVC, Steven Goodman (2003) writes, "This approach to critical literacy links media analysis to production; learning about the world is directly linked to the possibility of changing it. Command of literacy in this sense is not only a matter of performing well on standardized tests; it is a prerequisite for self-representation and autonomous citizenship" (p. 3).

Media production at REACH LA is more than just teaching isolated skills, it is part of a structured program based on key pedagogical practices that personalize and politicize the youth and their messages. Combining the analytical skills to deconstruct mainstream media with the artistic and technical skills to construct alternative counterhegemonic media becomes a natural process. In the *Computer-Active* and *Digital Arts-Active* programs, students learn video production, animation, digital arts, web site creation and maintenance, as well as the skills necessary to produce an annual teen magazine called *REACH for Me*. These technical skills incorporate their poetry, artwork, and short stories in public service campaigns for the larger goal of affecting change in their communities. Consistent with critical pedagogy, the students move from being objects of other people's research and media representations to becoming subjects empowered to tell their own stories and collectively challenge dominant oppressive myths. Goodman insists that "these possibilities can only be fully realized if the programs' guiding principles are based on a youth empowerment model; that is, teaching kids critical literacy requires that programs value and engage them as active participants in community problem-solving and as full partners in their own learning and growth" (p. 103).

REACH LA follows a Freirean problem-posing philosophy by helping students focus on problematic issues for them such as HIV/AIDS, homophobia, and racism. EVC has a different focus, yet a similar approach, as Goodman explains, "in addition to the myriad individual 'life skills' that are typically offered to at-risk kids, they need to be engaged in the study of the systemic roadblocks in their way—such as police brutality, unequal educational resources, substandard housing, and so on—and what sort of collective action they might take to move those roadblocks aside" (p. 3). It is these types of real-world connections that Dewey wrote about almost a century ago. This is the way to make education meaningful to students and empower them to become active participants necessary for radical democracy.

Media Education Abroad

Some of the oldest and best examples of media education are found outside the U.S., in countries such as Canada, New Zealand, Australia, and the U.K. There are also pockets of wonderful media literacy work occurring all over the world from Argentina to Hong Kong. This chapter does not offer an exhaustive analysis of media education in the world; however, some international perspective on media education is provided by focusing on the four countries that have spearheaded media education for several decades. A snapshot of a variety of media education programs around the world is also included.

One of the countries in the forefront of media literacy education is the U.S.'s neighbor to the north, Canada. The close proximity to the dominant global creator of media messages is one of the prime motivators for Canada's strong media education movement. Barry Duncan, the founding president of Ontario's Association for Media Literacy, asserts that the pervasiveness of U.S. popular culture is one of the major impetuses for spawning media education in Canada (Pungente & O'Malley, 1999, p. 228). John Pungente, Barry Duncan, and Neil Andersen (2005) write that "all provinces in Canada now include media literacy in the curriculum" (p. 140). Canada is one of the world leaders in media education for many reasons, not the least because Canadian educators have been involved in these issues since the 1960s. Over the years, they have developed a strong national Association for Media Literacy (AML), the Media Awareness Network (MNet), an online site that provides numerous resources for Canadian educators, and a "national mandate to include media literacy in the curriculum" (p. 147). Media education in Canada benefits greatly from the professional development support of the AML and production of media literacy resources by many of Canada's active media educators.[6]

In the lands down under, both New Zealand and Australia seem to have the most going on and the best support for media education in schools. Media teaching is thriving in New Zealand according to Geoff Lealand (2003). He writes:

> In recent years, teachers of media in New Zealand have been greatly advantaged through well-planned, official policy developments. There are the well-established Visual Language strand of the National English Curriculum, Media Studies as Unit Standards on the New Zealand Qualifications Framework, and the new National Certificate of Educational Achievement (NCEA). In addition to these formal structures, there are support systems for teachers (professional development workshops, for example), evidence of political support (the current Minister of Broadcasting is a former Media Studies lecturer), and more locally-developed resources. (p. 143)

For more than 20 years, critical media literacy has been institutionalized in the curriculum in Australia. Carmen Luke (1999) states that Australian education has basically institutionalized social justice issues in curriculum and practice. She describes an approach to media studies that reflects some of the more radical elements of feminism and multiculturalism. Luke writes, "From a social justice position, then, media analyses can show how inclusions and exclusions are structured in public discourse: the marginalisation, trivialisation, or romanticisation of indigenous Australians and other cultural minorities, gay persons and issues, rural groups, disabled persons, girls, and women" (p. 624). Barrie McMahon (1996) states that the successful maintenance of a radical approach necessitated a break between conservative traditions and education. He explains that as the pioneer teachers who shaped media education in Western Australia were learning with their students, issues of representation (especially of marginalized groups such as Aboriginal people) produced the edge that helped focus media studies on social injustice. This approach follows the principles of standpoint theory. Using ideas from other countries, Australian media educators designed student-centered curriculum that contextualized media studies within the framework of political economy, ideological struggle, control and ownership, and media policy. Robyn Quin suggests that the reason the Australians have been able to institutionalize the critical component with media education is because they began the process during the 1970s. At that time, in Australia, student activism and issues of social justice were very popular, thereby making it more acceptable to include social issues into the syllabus. She adds that once something becomes part of the official syllabus, it is extremely difficult to remove.[7] At the University of Queensland, in Australia, a teacher education program is combining information technology (IT) with media-cultural studies. Carmen Luke writes that their goal is to help new teachers use "IT as a tool with which to transform (a) the very relationships between student and teacher, among students, and between students and knowledge and (b) the very organisation of school knowledge itself" (2000a, p. 435). Alan Luke (2000) has also seen much success in Australia with critical literacy and the acceptance of the Four Resources Model.

In the U.K., media education has become institutionalized much more so than in the U.S., yet David Buckingham (2003) writes about his frustrations with media education in the U.K.: "there is still little more than a token recognition of its importance" (p. ix). Buckingham (2003, p. 93) states, "media educators have been inclined to regard the existence of a specialist Media Studies department as a prerequisite for the formulation—and particularly the *implementation*—of cross-curricular policies (see Robson, Simmons & Sohn-

Rethel, 1990). He writes, "Over the past twenty years, and particularly in the last ten, specialist Media Studies courses have experienced a steady growth in student numbers" (p. 87). But he admits that Media Studies, as stand alone courses in the U.K., "remains anything more than a minority subject: as an optional course, confined to the upper years of secondary school, it will only ever occupy a marginal role" (p. 88). Media Studies is not included "as a compulsory element of the National Curriculum." Buckingham writes that in the U.K., "there are identifiable elements of media education within the curriculum documents for areas such as History and Modern Languages, and most prominently within English—although whether and how such proposals are carried out in practice remains an open question" (p. 89). This seems very similar to what is happening in many of the state standards in the U.S. For example, in California from third to twelfth grade, elements of media literacy can be found in English, Social Studies, Science, Visual and Performing Arts, and the like. However, the U.K. is much more advanced than the U.S. since they have been doing this longer; they have more teacher training and have the option of Media Studies courses at the upper levels. There is also more of a sentiment in both the U.K. and Australia that media education is a "fundamental entitlement for all students" (p. 89). In 2003, the British government passed a Communications Act that is the first federal support for media literacy, and yet, this comes from the Ministry of Culture while the Department of Education still resists media education in the national curriculum (Buckingham, 2005).

In 2006, an alliance of academic and media organizations from eight European countries (Austria, Belgium, Britain, France, Germany, Portugal, Spain, and Sweden) launched the European Charter for Media Literacy. The group created a web site (http://www.euromedialiteracy.eu)[8] in which increasing numbers of individuals and organizations have been signing the six-point charter with the goal of encouraging media literacy in Europe. According to their web site, the European Charter for Media Literacy "exists to support the establishment of media literacy across Europe. By signing the Charter, organisations and individuals endorse a specific definition of media literacy, and commit to actions that will contribute to its development."

Outside of Europe, two small countries that have had a strong transformative focus in their media literacy curriculum have been Israel and South Africa. In Israel, the committee responsible for creating the national curriculum for media education identifies the need for a critical orientation in order "to advance citizen empowerment and progressive forms of social change," writes Dafna Lemish and Peter Lemish (1997, p. 222). In South Africa, many of Freire's ideas about emancipatory pedagogy have led to the development of media literacy curriculum that seeks to empower the disempowered and create "civic courage" (Criticos, 1997, p. 230). Civic courage grew out of resistance to the repressive forces of apartheid and requires critical literacy skills necessary for active citizenship in the information age. Costas Criticos of the South African Media Resource Center insists that civic courage does not emerge on its own (see Prinsloo & Criticos, 1991). He writes, "One way to develop this competence is to allow students as many opportunities as possible to wrestle with moral and social issues in simulations and discussions which allow free expressions and development of critical skills in a friendly and safe environment" (p. 237).

Many excellent books on media education have been printed in Spanish by the publishing house Ediciones de la Torre.[9] A coordinator and editor for this publishing project, Roberto Aparici, also runs an advanced degree program in New Technologies of Information and Communication at the National University of Distance Education (Universidad Nacional de Educación a Distancia) in Madrid, Spain. In Mexico, the National Pedagogical University (Universidad Pedagógica Nacional) created a high-quality media education program for training new teachers. They hired Aparici (1997) as their academic advisor to create an entire program for teaching media literacy to new teachers. The material created for this course, *Curso de Educación para los Medios*, contains an anthology of articles from leading experts in media literacy around the world, a series of magazines on the different core concepts of media literacy, a curriculum guide, videos, and audiotapes. The focus of this program, like media education in Spain and in other parts of Latin America, has much more of a critical edge than most media literacy in the U.S. Uruguayan Mario Kaplún (1998) writes that a pedagogy of communication should serve society as popular education to transform students and communities. From Argentina, Roxana Morduchowicz (2003) states, "Media education in Latin America must be, now and in the future, a space for a critical analysis and, at the same time, a site that allows students to move beyond the school towards their social engagement in the public life" (p. 71).

In Hong Kong, Alice Y. L. Lee (2003) writes, "In a very short time period, media education has gained momentum in this former British colony and by 2003, more than 200 schools and organizations in Hong Kong have conducted media education programs" (p. 149). She calls it a "multi-source voluntary grassroots movement" (p. 150). In Japan, Shin Mizukoshi and Yhei Yamauchi (2003) write,

> Media literacy itself is not the goal. Rather, like the larva for the butterfly, media literacy results in media practice. Through media practices, such as promotion of public

access, bridging the digital divide, extension of information technology to depopulated areas, and workshops using museums and community centers, citizens must be able to enrich their own communication activities and change the information society. (p. 166)

From media education happening in countries around the world, U.S. educators can learn much. There is also great potential for us to learn from our own. As was seen in the after-school programs on both coasts, there are some excellent examples of media education happening in the U.S. In the following chapter we hear the voices of a group of elementary school teachers who received federal funding to teach media literacy.

CHAPTER FOUR

Voices from the Trenches

Elementary School Teachers Speak about Implementing Media Literacy

For 3 years at the Leo Politi Elementary School in downtown Los Angeles, a federally funded project called SMARTArt taught teachers and students how to think critically about media and create alternative media messages. When Project SMARTArt ended in June 2004, the outside partner organizations left the teachers and the students to continue on their own. The Music Center discontinued sending artists to Leo Politi Elementary School; the Center for Media Literacy stopped providing professional development, coaching sessions, and demonstration lessons; and AnimAction ended their animation workshops at Leo Politi. Since the majority of the money from the grant was paying for these services of artists and professional development, when the grant ended so did most of the support. The equipment and material that was purchased with money from the grant remains at Leo Politi, although only a small portion of the funding went toward purchasing equipment and resources, such as two televisions and VCRs, a couple of digital cameras, a computer for the animation software, and supplies like videos and books. Many of those items have been dispersed or are unaccounted for.

Some of the resources that were developed or used during the grant have been posted on the Internet, such as media literacy lesson plans, a theoretical framework for how to teach media literacy and a case study about Project SMARTArt.[1] During the 3 years, approximately 850 students received lessons in media literacy and the arts and about 25 teachers (two noncredentialed after-school teachers) received between 1 and 3 years of professional development in media literacy and the four visual and performing arts (dance, music, theater, and visual arts).

As part of my research into searching for the best ways to bring critical media literacy to elementary school students, I interviewed many of the teachers who participated in Project SMARTArt. In 2006, approximately 2 years after the grant ended, I interviewed 14 of the 23 credentialed teachers who participated for either 1, 2, or 3 years of the grant. I investigated what these teachers think about media literacy in 2006, as they reflected on their past and present experiences learning about it and teaching it to their students. The ways and degrees to which these teachers are currently using what they learned from the grant varies across the board, yet all spoke about the importance of media literacy while also admitting to a sharp decrease in implementation of media literacy since the grant ended.

This research has allowed me to listen to the voices of teachers in the trenches, the ones who know schooling best from their firsthand experience, yet they are seldom consulted when policy decisions are made or school reform is enacted. In this chapter, I present and analyze some of the comments and concerns expressed by these teachers. All the names have been changed with pseudonyms in order to provide anonymity (see Appendix C for more information about each teacher).

I arranged a formal interview with each teacher individually for about an hour, either in their classroom or some private space. The three questions that guided this research are (a) What are the best ways to integrate critical media literacy into elementary school curriculum? (b) What aspects of critical media literacy (key questions, core concepts, democratic pedagogy, etc.) are most useful and why? (c) What obstacles keep educators from teaching critical media literacy? More specific questions that were used as an informal interview guide can be found in Appendix D.

All the interviews were tape-recorded and transcribed. Each transcription was then sent to the interviewee for him or her to check what he or she had said and make any corrections or changes. A couple people responded with minor suggestions and all their changes were adhered to. The transcripts were then reviewed and coded as to the themes that I noticed recurring or patterns that seemed pertinent. As new questions arose, I recontacted teachers via telephone or email. I also interviewed two administrators (the new principal and one of the two assistant principals) to explore further some of the teachers' comments. After repeated readings of all the interviews, dominant themes emerged into which I have divided this chapter. The first deals with the belief that all the teachers shared about the importance of media literacy in elementary school. Next, different types of media literacy are presented and grouped into three of the four approaches to media education as described in Chapter Two. Using examples, the differences and similarities between these approaches are illustrated. The third theme deals with new obstacles, at Leo Politi and beyond, that are impeding and, at times, intimidating many of the teachers from teaching media literacy. Finally, suggestions from the teachers about what they think is necessary for media literacy to flourish in elementary school is explored.

Since a major focus of Project SMARTArt involved training teachers so that they would teach their students, I decided not to talk with students nor attempt to assess student learning. My focus with this research is on the teachers in an attempt to learn what they think is the most effective way to assist them to teach media literacy and/or critical media literacy to their students.

The Importance of Media Literacy

The most common sentiment from all 14 SMARTArt teachers interviewed was a belief in the importance of media literacy. Although they were not formally asked if they believed media education was important, all of the teachers offered their views about the value and need for media literacy. Various reasons for their support of media literacy were expressed, yet most commented on the need for students to think critically about media since it surrounds them all the time.

Third-grade teacher Mr. Baker wrote in an email, "I feel that media literacy needs to be taught at least as much if not more than the basics of reading and math. Everything builds on it. Understanding that every message that is coming at them has a reason, will help them. The more they understand the concept, and if they don't have the background, i.e. elementary, they will have a harder time with those concepts later." By framing media literacy concepts as essential building blocks, Mr. Baker positions media literacy as a major paradigm shift for education.

Special education teacher Mr. Shaw suggested that media literacy is important because it teaches metacognitive skills in thinking about thinking. He said that media literacy is important "because it teaches kids how to think critically for themselves and apply the essential questions to everything in life.

Who sent the message? Why did they send it? Who is this targeted to? Are there any biases? It teaches them how to think and I think, isn't that what we're in business to do, to teach kids how to think for themselves." He connects media literacy with social justice through teaching empathy. He said, "I think when you teach a person to think for themselves and think outside of the social box that they may live in, in terms of their family unit, in terms of their cultural unit, in terms of how they were brought up, I think if you teach them how to question what has been presented to them in their life, they will be able to see things from an empathetic point of view and step into other people's shoes." The connection of critical thinking with empathy that Mr. Shaw mentions is essential for critical media literacy and the goal of critical solidarity (Ferguson, 2001).

Teaching students how to deconstruct a media message is something that second-grade teacher Ms. Vargas stated helps students "know what was involved in the creation of that message. Just being able to have higher level thinking skills about what that message is, whether it's advertisement or news media or newspapers, anything that carries a message, you are able to step away from just reacting to it, you take into account what your reaction is, but you step away from it and you look at it analytically and see what was involved in constructing it and what was the reason for it and who the target audience was and what [was] the objective; you're able to think about that message critically." In her description of media literacy, Ms. Vargas expresses a perspective that looks critically at media, that moves away from censorship and protection toward empowerment and analysis. She stated, "I think because media is just such a part of our society, you can totally get swallowed in that whole world if you don't stop, step back and say, 'OK, there's a reason why they're doing that and I have to be aware so I can make a more educated choice.' The whole concept of stepping out of that box and looking at the overall picture—if anything, that's what I've taken away from media literacy training."

Special education teacher Ms. Hendrix also believes that media literacy is important to help both students and teachers start "thinking out of the box." She suggested that everyone should be "more self-reflective in one's interpretation of media. Opening up more dialogue to access that, from not only the kids, but ourselves." Ms. Hendrix's comments align with bell hooks's ideas "that teachers must be actively committed to a process of self-actualization that promotes their own wellbeing if they are to teach in a manner that empowers students" (hooks, 1994, p. 15). Awareness and engagement with media are now necessary elements of 21st-century self-actualization. Third-grade teacher Ms. Martin commented that media literacy is important for her to think more critically about media so that her students can look at media differently. "I think the biggest value was that I had this new wealth of knowledge about media that I had not had before. Just looking at media in ways that I had never looked at, and taking that perspective and working with my students. I knew this instinctively, but the fact that there are corporations with their own agendas and that they create this media and there are purposes for that. I didn't know that. To have that knowledge, to be able to teach students that these things exist, and to have them come back to me after a lesson and then when they went home, they would look at media, or they would look at a commercial, and they would say, 'Oh, I know this, or I noticed that.' Maybe if they were watching a TV show and they saw a Coke ad or something, they started looking at media differently."

Teaching students that all media are constructed is a challenge for third-grade teacher Mr. Gomez, who stated that often students don't realize media messages are constructed by people for particular purposes. Mr. Gomez commented that it is important for students to know "there is always a different viewpoint to something. What you think is fact is actually someone else's version of the facts." He said that students should learn to apply this concept "to a lot of things, even textbooks," since often people "think it's fact, just because it's in a textbook." Mr. Gomez stated, "I remember we went to a workshop at the Center [for Media Literacy] somewhere and they were showing how news clips or media is a reflection of the person reporting the news. Also, how music and camera angles can change the effect it has on a person. You add scary music, then you feel scared and creeped-out. Where if you remove it, it doesn't have as much effect on you . . . the information is someone else's viewpoint and it's affecting you, they're controlling you in a funny . . . subtle or indiscreet way, they are controlling you. Controlling what you know, so you have to be critical of what information you're receiving, don't just take it for fact."

A wonderful example of fourth-grade students internalizing a media literacy frame of mind is told by Mr. Ruiz. He explains, "I know that group of kids got it because near the end, we received a big pack in the mail. There was a big pack of free book covers, something like *Madagascar*, some movie for kids . . . we had talked about billboards and advertising and how much it costs, and one of the kids said to me, 'Well, are they giving us anything else for advertising?' I said, 'No, they just think that by giving you a free book cover, it's . . .' 'But we're doing free advertising for them.' I said, 'Exactly!' So he came to that conclusion and then I said, 'Find a solution, what can you do?' 'But, it's good paper,' they said and it really is. They came to the conclusion of flipping it over and drawing their own. So the advertising went inside and they drew their own, it was really neat." Mr. Ruiz used this example to demonstrate how his media literacy lessons had led to the goal of media education that Len Masterman (1994) calls *critical autonomy*, the ability and desire to think critically without prompting by the teacher. Mr. Ruiz's students had recognized that they were being used by advertisers to promote a movie for free through the mere donation of book covers. They not only perceived the manipulation but they counteracted it by appropriating the material for their own purposes. Mr. Ruiz said that this example was just one of many where he was able to see his students developing their critical consciousness. Mr. Ruiz stated, "We talked about the advertising around here and we get alcohol advertising so much more here than in other higher affluent communities. They were becoming much more aware sooner than I expected or sooner than the other kids around."

Special education teacher Ms. Brown focused largely on advertising and stated that media literacy is important because it helps make students "more aware of what's going on out there and how companies use color and music and so many different things just to entice them." She commented that her students "became much more aware of their environment. Just something as simple as walking down the street, they understood, Oh, look at that billboard, what is that billboard trying to tell you? What do they want you to do? And I really do think they became much more savvy consumers. Whereas before, I don't think these things even registered. And even something like talking about commercials. I would have them watch commercials on Saturday and they would count how many were about toys, how many were about cereal, for example, and we talked about that. I had them watch a show that I would watch, something that they could watch and then they would come back and tell me what kind of commercials were for my age group or what would be considered my age group. And we talked about that and some of them became really sharp because they realized as it got closer to Christmas, even if it was adult shows, all of a sudden some of it would be toy kind of commercials. So, they were trying to hit up the person who was going to buy the toys." As Ms. Brown's students developed their awareness of media and understanding of how advertising targets audiences, they were learning concrete examples of abstract concepts about textual analysis, audience theory, and political economy.

When second-grade teacher Ms. Rogers compared the difference between her second-grade students now (who receive almost no media literacy) and her students during the grant (who received regular media literacy lessons), she expressed her belief that media literacy helped her students better understand the inquiry process. When asked if she believes that her students developed better questions because of media literacy, she responded, "I saw it more then.

Now, I'm still teaching my kids about questions. But I think media literacy really helped them understand what a question was and how to really pose a question. They were more expressive . . . I saw more of it then when I was really doing the media literacy than now." By using a media literacy framework based on an inquiry process, Ms. Rogers was able to empower her students to critically question not only media but also all communication. Mr. Baker insisted that media literacy can help students understand the power of media and how to use probing questions to analyze messages. He believes that "kids will do better in testing when they understand things better."

The question of what is developmentally appropriate raised some interesting responses from a few teachers. Ms. Hendrix stated that she believes media literacy is "absolutely developmentally appropriate [for elementary school students] and should actually be emphasized as early as possible, because the kids are at that developmental stage where they're highly impressionable and they start to develop these skill sets in their thinking. Things start to really develop internally, they build these neurological pathways, they just get in these behaviors and belief systems and so, yes, kids should have media literacy as well as financial literacy, and the like—literacy in general. They should be exposed to whatever formal literacy helps them to be more Socratic, more critical in their thinking, absolutely. It's a social injustice if we're waiting until they're older to try to unravel all the junk that builds up. Then it's way harder because the filters are that much more ingrained." This call for many literacies as early as possible echoes Kellner's assertion that technological and multicultural changes now require we re-vision education to embrace *multiple literacies*. He writes, "multiple literacies include not only media and computer literacies, but also a diverse range of social and cultural literacies, ranging from ecoliteracy (e.g., understanding the body and environment) to economic and financial literacy to a variety of other competencies that enable us to live well in our social worlds" (Kellner, 2006a, p. 261).

Although most of the teachers' comments tended to agree with Ms. Hendrix's previous sentiments about the developmentally appropriateness of media literacy, two teachers did mention that perhaps social justice issues of critical media literacy might not be appropriate for the lower elementary school age students. Second-grade teacher Ms. Ramirez said, "In the lower grades, I don't know. I would be hesitant to say, depending on the topic obviously, but I don't think the kids are making those deeper connections about social justice or they don't really have a concrete understanding of it until they get into 4th or even 5th grade. Some, even in 5th grade, but I definitely think it should be an important role. I don't think that media literacy is without those issues. I think they're embedded in there, whether or not you take them out for kids to analyze, I think they're embedded. It should be taught. It should be part of the curriculum, it should be, they should address it some way, but not in the very lowest grades." Third-grade teacher Mr. Harvey was also hesitant about teaching social justice to students in the early elementary grades because "there is such a thing as life experience, eight years is not very much." While it is important to be developmentally appropriate, Mr. Harvey's comments tend to reflect a deficit approach that undervalues the wealth of knowledge young children bring with them, especially about issues related to media.

When fourth-grade teacher Ms. Jones was asked if she thought elementary school age children were ready to learn about media literacy, she replied, "Well, whether they're ready or not, for their own protection they better start learning something about it because they're turned into the media in a different way than any other generation has been and they can get the bad messages and the good messages all the time. They're going to have to have a better way of, at a younger age, to be able to evaluate what they're able to get into and a lot of the negative things that are coming in their way." She insisted that "it's gonna continue, its not going to slow down . . . To be able to talk to people anywhere in the world and be able to get information about anything without opening a book and be able to have conversations with people that have likes, likenesses that you have so that you can advance in your thinking and skills. It could be good or bad." The assertion that we live in a different time and education needs to address these changes in society is also an argument that is being made by many advocates promoting information literacy (McClure, 1993), new literacies (Kist, 2005), and 21st-century skills (Partnership for the 21st century).

Mr. Harvey and Ms. Ramirez commented on the constant bombardment of advertising on children and how it creates a need for media literacy. Ms. Ramirez suggested that children must be taught about advertising and much more. She said, "I do think it's [media literacy] an important aspect that children have to learn because I think that we need to make them more aware and metacognitive about advertising, what we look at every day, what we see every day and how it functions in our society, whether it's news, whether it's movies, whether it's a video game, whether it's a poster, whether it's a billboard, just making children conscientious of the messages that we're receiving, not just as advertising messages, but even in the news. It does help them become more aware and make better choices, what they're going to buy, or how they're going to act."

Especially Special Education

During interviews with the four special education teachers, they often mentioned problems related to the marginalization of special education within the public school. At Leo Politi we were lucky to have several special education classes and even more fortunate to have most of them participate in the media literacy grant. Listening to the special education teachers has brought out just how important it is that media literacy is not something that only general education students receive. Special education teachers commented on how often their students are forgotten or assumptions are made about what they can or cannot do. These interviews and the experiences during 3 years of the grant make a strong argument that students in special education can benefit greatly from media literacy for many reasons.

Ms. Brown commented, "I think honestly, it was really quite an honor to be part of the grant. It really was nice because so many times I feel that my children are just left out of things and I really felt that they had an opportunity to be treated like every other child that goes to school. I think, in terms of teaching, I really had to focus on some things, not necessarily re-think things, but it really gave me an opportunity, as a teacher, to do things that I never thought to do. I didn't even know I could do them and it gave me opportunities to sneak other activities in, which were educational, for example, we did a lot of advertising and all. I never would have thought to use that, in terms of homework assignments, or even reading or spelling, but it gave them chances to do it and they didn't see a lot of that as work. They really saw a lot of that as just fun. They didn't really get that they were working."

Since media pedagogy is multimodal and experiential, it helps overcome some of the limitations of a single modality as well as lowers the affective filters (Krashen, 1995) that create invisible barriers for children acquiring a new language or with special needs, be they physical, mental, or social. Mr. Shaw offered an example where lowering the affective filters gave his students more of a level playing field than they usually had when mixing with regular education students. He spoke about his former students, "they become just normal kids without having to think about the burden of being understood when they speak . . . [Sandy] had a really tough time speaking and communicating just basic needs, like having to go to the bathroom or being hungry, so when he was able to be that tiger when [the drama teacher] came in, he wasn't a kid with special needs anymore, he became a tiger . . . And they interacted with their general ed peers, you could really see the confidence level, especially [Sandy], increase because he was more talkative, he understood that he could be something else." Mr. Shaw also spoke about media literacy activities with music, "I also saw that again when they were playing the instruments with [the music teacher]. They didn't have to talk, they didn't have to communicate any needs. All they did was pound on those instruments and again, it takes all of the affective filters and it diminishes them to a point where everybody is the same; extremely powerful."

Ms. Hendrix commented on the ability for media literacy to help her students improve their critical thinking skills. She stated, "The kids I had at that time, many of them had significant speech/language impairments and learning disabilities. They definitely started to demonstrate an increased level of critical thinking and expression. Definitely with some of the activities . . . they started making really great connections and they were definitely better critical thinkers." For example, Ms. Hendrix mentioned, "one activity was when the elections were coming up and there was all the campaigning going on. What I would have the kids do when we went to the computer lab was to find the latest photographs of the election and the kids had to express their impressions of why they're going to vote for who. Why they would vote for Kerry or why they would vote for Bush, based on the images they were looking at and the captions that they could read. I abstained from reading too much to them because I really wanted them to focus just on the images and we built this kind of portfolio or this album of images and we kept pictures of Bush and Kerry. It was amazing how, from week to week, their perceptions of these individuals would change, based on the images that they were looking at. For example, students would express perceptions such as, 'Bush was a good guy cause he was with the animals in that other picture, but this week, he's with some military,' you know like some person in the army or something. So that was really amazing, I thought. It's how they started to look. Or I was able to pose questions to them about what does what or where somebody is, the setting that they're in, or who they're with or what they're doing, why does that make you think a certain way about a person? They would definitely get very, very excited about voting for one or the other and then when they started to see how they were changing their minds, that was pretty neat because they were questioning . . . I think (hope) it had some lasting impressions for some of them. To witness their oral skills and critical thinking skills increase was exciting."

Developing critical thinking skills is an important goal of media literacy, yet the inclusion of art education with media literacy also holds great value for all students, especially special education students. Ms. Brown spoke about her special education class, "I think for my children, it was really nice because [for] some of the students I had those years, reading was so hard for them and math was so hard and it gave them opportunities to be successful. It was really nice because when they would do it with general ed children, you couldn't tell who was who … like one year I had some that were just wonderful artists and it was just such a nice opportunity for them because when they worked down in the multi-purpose room and everyone was drawing, they were like, [David] do this, [David] do this. It was so nice for [David] to really see that he had a talent and that other children actually could notice it. It was just so nice for them to have those chances to shine in other areas that maybe they couldn't. Like when they had the music person when [the music teacher] came, that some of them had wonderful rhythm and really could. They loved it, we made the instruments, we played the instruments, we used with our words, like for syllables and it gave them a chance to be successful, it wasn't just, how many syllables? Four, they actually could play it on their instrument and get it. In a way, they thought they were having fun, but they really did learn a lot and it was really nice for them and nice for me to have another way to teach them and for them to understand something." The ability of media literacy and art education to make learning fun and pleasurable should not be underestimated, especially as dropout rates increase.

Special education teacher Ms. Smith stated that media literacy was such a wonderful way to integrate students. "I think it's great because it's multi-level. You can do it with a variety of ages and it's just multi-abilities. Not everybody has to be reading at the same level to do a lot of these activities. So, I think it provides a lot of great mainstreaming activities, mixing activities." Although many of these benefits could also apply to art education without any of the media literacy layers, Ms. Smith also spoke about other values of media literacy for her special education students, such as exploring the politics of representation and how her students see themselves being represented. Ms. Smith explained that she and her students talk "extensively about how we communicate with others and I think because we are dealing with a disabled population, we talk about self-image and how you want others to perceive you." Ms. Smith analyzed with her students the fact that people with disabilities are often underrepresented or misrepresented in mainstream media. While her students were investigating the scarcity of images of senior citizens in mainstream media, they also noticed "the fact that they [children with physical disabilities] were in magazines that were focusing on equipment," commented Ms. Smith. By teaching students about the politics of representation they become better prepared to question these types of inequalities as choices made by individuals for specific reasons. Being able to reject the "commonsense" notion that media are neutral or natural allows students the framework to position their own identities on their own terms and reject discriminatory representations of themselves and others.

The importance of media literacy can also be seen in Ms. Smith's comments about her new attitude with media tools. Ms. Smith said, "I think empowering them with tools, I'm thinking back then [during the grant] when, like now, I don't think twice about handing a kid a camera, where before I did. That's something that changed me a lot, it's giving them more opportunities to do things and I really think that was a big thing. I was thinking, are they going to be able to, do they know what, talking about the video camera too, it's more use of the equipment, the tripod. I'm thinking I still have the tripod here, it really empowered them, those are like an adult toy. You know, a lot of parents say, No, you don't touch that. On top of that, using a wheelchair and being able to use something like that, why shouldn't they? I think that was really something that I feel made an impact on me, made me think differently."

When Ms. Brown was asked if elementary age students could handle media literacy, she replied, "They definitely could. Even though, when you worked on the questions and you had maybe an upper level set of questions, then you had questions that are at a different level. But my children definitely understood those questions and we had them posted and it wasn't like we didn't have to go over it, but they understood what was happening. Maybe they didn't have the vocabulary . . . But, I don't see any reason why it can't be something at the elementary schools. Even some of those kinder children, they produced wonderful things." Ms. Smith agreed and suggested, "you have to look at things and scaffold them and just kind of break it down to what they can do. Everybody can contribute something."

Different Types of Media Education

In Chapter Two, I discussed Douglas Kellner's division of approaches to media education into four camps: protectionist, media literacy movement, arts education, and critical media literacy. Even though the differences between these approaches are less distinct in the lower grades, they are general tendencies that reflect various perspectives about media and education. They also reveal the content and quality of teaching practices. While focusing on the differences, it is important to remember that these are not clear-cut restricted categories, instead they are a collection of porous tendencies. Since the goal of this research is to encounter best practices for teaching critical media literacy in elementary school, the critical media literacy approach is being positioned as the preferred approach to media education on the grounds that it is most suited for promoting transformative pedagogy and radical democracy.

Kellner's four categories are cumulative approaches, often like a pyramid, building on each other rather than a linear progression of separate ideas. In this pyramid analogy, critical media literacy is at the top since it incorporates ideas from the other three approaches. The approach with the least to offer the pyramid is the protectionist because it is based on a negative view of the media and a limited view of the audience's potential to negotiate alternative readings. It can contribute to spreading awareness of media as influential and worthy of analysis and critique. The art education approach offers a useful base that can open education to be more experiential, multimodal, creative, fun, and expressive. The integration of the media literacy movement core concepts with arts education helps push the arts education to be more critical and deepen the potential for critical thinking. The final layer, critical media literacy, provides a problem-posing pedagogy that addresses issues of social justice that can be individually and socially empowering and transformative.

The majority of the 14 teachers interviewed tend to embody a media literacy movement perspective that aims to proactively empower students to analyze and create media as a way of developing cognitive critical thinking skills. Though this was the most common approach, aspects of three of the four types of media education can be found in the interviews. Protectionist fears of the negative effects of violence on TV and in video games were voiced once or twice, yet none of the teachers promoted a negative attitude toward media or partook in media bashing. The relative absence of the protectionist approach to media literacy is notable. Some teachers viewed media literacy similar to art education—a fun experiential tool useful for creative expression and livening up other subjects. However, most of the interviews reflect a solid media literacy education perspective engaging core concepts of cultural studies and expanding print literacy to be more inclusive of other forms of communication. Finally, just a handful of teachers explicitly engaged in critical media literacy by addressing issues of power, inequality, and social justice.

Teaching media literacy can be a major paradigm shift for many teachers; it requires movement from a psychological model of education to a sociological one. Alan Luke and Peter Freebody compare differences between these two models by suggesting that the more common psychological model of reading is one in which natural processes are more important than cultural practices, the text is considered a neutral conveyer of information as opposed to being embedded with ideological reading and writing positions, and the goals favor decoding, comprehension and personal growth over pragmatics, critique, cultural action and social identity (1997, p. 207). This means that a sociological model has less focus on individual cognitive development and more incorporation of the social contexts of the student and the content being taught. Much like Luke and Freebody's Four Resource Model (1999), a sociological model of literacy requires multiple practices, and critical media literacy should be one of them. Many teachers are not used to thinking of popular culture and media as being important to education. Therefore, encouraging teachers to broaden their definition of literacy can be a first step in this movement toward a sociological model. A next step should be to deepen critical thinking in relation to social and cultural contexts, and for this, one can benefit greatly from engagement with cultural studies concepts, something with which many teachers are unfamiliar. These include textual analysis using semiotics and visual literacy, audience theory, and the importance of different readings versus dominant readings, as well as ideology and issues of bias as they conflict with assumptions of objectivity. Cultural studies also critiques political economy, institutional influences, and the commercial purposes of entertainment and media, which is often absent from teaching that involves mass media (i.e., journalism, music, documentaries, etc.). These ideas emerge from an overarching understanding that all media and information are socially constructed.

For some, critical media literacy puts human rights before property rights, and concerns for social justice challenge corporate free market ideologies. This pedagogy encourages empathy and an openness to explore the hierarchical relationships of power in communication that benefit and disadvantage individuals and groups. It also involves the process of critical inquiry to unveil the way social systems function in perpetuating themselves and reproducing the status quo. Critical media literacy is transformative pedagogy that aims to empower students to take action that counteracts and challenges the problems they encounter, thus connecting themselves in *critical solidarity* with the world around them.

Art Education and Media Literacy

Many academics have written about the importance of pleasure in media studies and education (Buckingham, 2003; Mission & Morgan, 2006). Ms. Jones values media literacy for making school more fun and allowing for more creativity. While Ms. Jones's interview reflects an arts education approach most of the time, she did mention the need for schools to promote critical thinking. In the following quote, she discusses a claymation class that her teenage grandson attended outside of school. "They were so interested in having a good time that that [critical analysis] wasn't something that had to be part of what they were doing. It worked a lot better after they've done a project and you give them something, a question to reflect on in their journal and then a time to discuss what they've put in . . . you have to guide that. It's not going to happen otherwise automatically." Focusing on the media literacy work at Leo Politi, Ms. Jones suggested that the importance of school can be to move the art education into a bigger perspective. Ms. Jones stated, "That was one thing I thought was really nice with all the discussion that the students had. School rooms seem to be a safe place where they can give their true opinions and accept what other people said about theirs. I didn't see a lot of ruffled feathers and somebody said, I don't think that's what you meant to do, because that didn't tell me that's what you were thinking, or say, that was really great, I never thought of that. The fact that they had a peer audience and their own voice was really nice."

Ms. Jones commented that she believes media literacy "improved my skills in teaching and things that were presented in dance, in drama, made me more aware of the fact how exciting it was for kids and how nice it was for them to be able to do a new skill, like a cartoon, drawing." She also commented that the open pedagogy often also found in art education gave her students "a much broader look at how to evaluate something because it gave them some clues, like look at the color, where was it taken? who was it for? a lot of open-ended questions. A lot of open-ended teaching. Then there was a lot of discussion and a lot of opinions and they were all acceptable; something different. This opened their eyes in a different way and it took them a while because, they really didn't know what we were talking about." Through fun art activities, Ms. Jones's students were learning new clues and skills that were helping them develop abilities to think inferentially.

Having students act out a school play is typical performing arts education and can be a lot of fun, yet never engage with media literacy concepts or critical questions. Several SMARTArt teachers spoke about plays their students performed and how they tried to make those media literacy productions. Second-grade teachers Ms. Rogers and Ms. Hernandez often combine their classes to perform an OCR story.[2] Ms. Rogers mentioned that they applied the media literacy concepts, but there is often not much time for both analysis and production. During the grant, Mr. Harvey had his students perform the story of the Bionic Bunny, based on a book (Brown & Brown, 1984) that exposes the constructed nature of media superheroes. By beginning with a topic that looked critically at media, the performance embodied media literacy concepts. Mr. Harvey also had his students create other media to go along with the play, such as advertising and invitations.

The potential of arts education to integrate well with media literacy was apparent from the grant. When Ms. Rogers was asked if the Arts Prototype teacher, who comes into her class now, teaches the kids to be critical about art, she replied, "I don't think she's very critical about it, it's just like it's part of the art. But I see it as an opportunity to say a few words." Ms. Rogers feels that Arts Prototype is so related to media literacy that "it could be put together and really work very well together." She said, "To me, it's so close that you could take the art part and just add the critical questions of media literacy."

Integrating Media Literacy across the Curriculum

In elementary school, there are basically two options for teaching media literacy: one is as a separate subject in addition to the mandated curriculum and the other is to integrate it with subjects that the teacher is already required to cover. Since time is so limited and the expectations of what to teach are so great, most SMARTArt teachers tried to integrate media literacy concepts and questions into their curriculum in many different ways. Mr. Baker told about how he uses the chart from the Center for Media Literacy (see Appendix A) with the key questions. He said, "I have my chart with the questions to reference them. The primary way that I reference them is, especially at the end of each story that we read in Open Court, I review those questions and I ask the kids to address those questions for that story that we've read. They usually don't get to all of them, they usually don't, I have to push them really hard to get to more than, who gave the message and how did they present it, and why did they present it? Get into how could other people interpret it differently, that's something that rarely gets addressed."

During the SMARTArt professional development, some specific media literacy lessons were taught, yet the emphasis of the training focused more on integrating media literacy rather than teaching it as a separate subject. This is probably easiest in elementary school, where all subjects are taught by the same teacher and curriculum integration is often encouraged. During the grant, Ms. Hernandez integrated media literacy throughout her curriculum and into her students' homes. For homework, she still has her students do the equivalent of a book report for a television show. She said, they "have to sit with their parent and watch a show. Not only watch it and just be passive, but actually go into it and say, who are the characters, what was the problem, what was the solution within the show?" Since the grant ended, Ms. Hernandez no longer does many of her media literacy lessons, yet this homework assignment continues. Ms. Hernandez remarked, "I still do it because it's such a good way for them to see that people use media, but they also use stories and the story board and the story element to create a show. They enjoy it and television is just so much part of their lives. So, I figured why not go and tell the parents, this is a good way for you to analyze the shows that your kids are watching and make sure that they're watching something that's good for them instead of something that's not going to be any benefit to them. The parents enjoy that homework a lot, so I still do it."

Ms. Ramirez spoke about how she now uses media differently than before the grant. She said, "I point out to children things that I didn't realize before. I've always used [media], even magazines, in making up collages, but now I go more into depth as to the photography and the way that media uses different angles in their photography to prove certain points and so I remember that you had one [lesson] with Arnold Schwarzenegger[3] and that's one I brought up several times, even after I left the classroom. I actually brought this one up and I did a little training, just a tiny little training to show the children how they're the same people, but they're shown differently. In certain illustrations, where you can point things out like that, I will do that. Like, look the man looks really small, but is he really small? I try to incorporate it, but it's not a specific lesson, you kind of just move on. But I do something that I didn't do before, and so that's what I incorporate now, I have them look for specifics, look for camera angles, look for the lighting, is it dark, is it light, is it to evoke different emotions. How photography evokes different emotions depending on how something is photographed." The way Ms. Ramirez now includes visual literacy skills in her language arts lessons reflects a more expanded notion of literacy that is closer in line with the multimodal avenues through which students are receiving information now. This more open understanding of literacy is an important aspect of media literacy and a necessary beginning for critical media literacy.

Ms. Martin commented on how teaching media literacy has become a natural part of her teaching, and she now incorporates it incidentally. Ms. Martin spoke about the challenge, "My biggest concern, and probably the concern of almost every teacher, was how do I fit this into what I already have to do, because there's so much to do. I think what was eased [during the grant] was that there was no pressure. It's not that you have to do everything. It's that you learn all these things and that it was okay for them to become sort of integrated into the program; to just happen naturally. And it did, and I was in it for three years, a full three years, and it has become a part of my natural planning and decisions and that's been really good." She said, "I'll notice we can talk about symbols, we can use newspapers images, we can use imagination, we talk about how these images are created when we were looking at magazine images. So definitely, all these things are being used, just not as systematic as it used to be, but it's there. It's in my head, and so I'm using it. That's good and the kids are getting it. It's probably easier. And I think that's how we need to do things anyways. It just kind of is integrated and it just kind of happens naturally. When I'm planning, I can say, oh I can do media literacy here, we can talk about one of the media questions. It happens, it's just not as structured as it was before." While Ms. Martin's natural incorporation of media literacy concepts and questions into her teaching lacks a structured approach, its profound understanding allows for a more dynamic application that can be applied to any educational program or fad that too often comes and goes.

Mr. Ruiz told about a lesson where he combined popular culture and media literacy with a math lesson. He said, "Just last week I received my renewal for Time Magazine and ... it didn't give me a total of how much the subscription was, but I know there was a [subscription card] you get 58 issues for 63 cents, but it didn't tell me the total and it bothered me because I needed to see a total so I used that for example. I brought Time magazine in and had the kids try to figure out and I decided to go through some magazines and cut out the subscription ads and realized that was a way that I can use it in Math and we ended up doing a little project where they each got one. I was able to steal some from a store magazine rack, enough to make their own little poster and talk about it, and that the intention was to really lure you in to getting the magazine. Off the rack it's $3.95 but for you, 52 cents, you get 37 of them, but it didn't give you a total." This is an excellent example of a real-world connection to math and media literacy concepts. Mr. Ruiz brought into the classroom an experience from his personal life that involved popular media and a math problem for his students to wrestle with authentic applications for abstract concepts (Dewey, 1916/1997).

Ms. Hendrix spoke about how she tries to bring popular culture into the classroom as a way of helping her students connect with the material. She said, "I try to help kids access, if they're reading a story, let's say about friendship, I say, let's connect that to some popular media character that relates to something you're reading. So, I try to make those kinds of connections." Another example of teachers using items from popular culture as texts to read and analyze happens every year when teachers Ms. Rogers, Ms. Hernandez, and Ms. Smith have their students analyze messages on t-shirts. This current year began with a bit of a protectionist approach by some of the teachers. Ms. Rogers explained, "I saw some t-shirts around the school that the kids were wearing that were like, Oh my, do they know what that shirt says? I don't remember what it was, but some of them were like curse words, or something. You know criminal, something about criminals." This became a media literacy lesson as the teachers and students brought in t-shirts from home that had writing on them and they talked about them and the issues and people represented on the shirts. During this lesson, the students designed their own t-shirts and logos and had to explain what they were about. In past years, students have made t-shirts to promote a cause, like saving the whales. Ms. Rogers commented on how the lesson was creative and fun while also educational as the t-shirts and logos took them into all sorts of cultural and social issues.

Social Justice and Critical Media Literacy

Ms. Vargas felt that media literacy is good for building bridges with social studies. She stated, "A lot of present problems could have been prevented if we would have learned from our mistakes in the past. So maybe looking at history, looking at different periods and using media literacy as that bridge between, yes, this is an event in history, let's say the Civil Rights Movement, and then having media literacy be that bridge to what's going on presently and using the messages that we see today, that we receive today, what's a part of our society, our environment, our immediate neighborhood, where do we see, maybe not the exact same thing, but the essence of it, how it does still exist today. Right off the bat, I'm thinking always looking at social studies, history, the social sciences for that."

Although Mr. Ruiz is not able to teach a lot about social justice these days, he believes that using media literacy can be a great way to expose his students to issues of social injustice. He commented, "just last week during ML King [celebrations], the kids were learning that it wasn't just . . . a black issue. I asked the kids, here's a picture of a water fountain, Colored Only and Whites Only, where would you drink? All the kids think they were able to drink from the White Fountain, just because they're not black. Defining what colored means and I found some old, old newspapers that have copies of older newspapers during the time of the boycott and Rosa Parks and the kids were able to make that connection, that they're colored. When they mean colored, they don't mean the Blacks, because they think they could walk through that front door, they think they'd be able to drink out of the White Only fountain, so, very little social justice but I think through media literacy it would be a great way; easier and more fun. I mean the kids would just enjoy it. You can integrate so much, you can integrate art and take care of a couple of standards, couple of subjects all in one."

Many teachers would probably bring issues of social justice into their class-room if they felt more comfortable with how to teach them. When teachers don't know *how* to teach a subject matter, especially a sensitive one like racism, sexism, or homophobia, they tend to avoid it. Ms. Ramirez agreed that teaching social justice issues is "definitely the most responsible thing for us to do as teachers. If we are teaching media literacy, we teach all aspects of it, including the racism, the unfairness, the social class, the differences in social class, but how?" Mr. Harvey stated, "Stereotypes, yep, yep. Stereotyping, yeh. Umm, although I didn't really FOCUS on, I mean I didn't emphasize that TOO much. Umm, but, I didn't know where to go with it. OK, so you have the stereotype right. We did a little bit of that when you came in and and talked about the newspaper ads and we talked about differences of males and females. W . . . e . . .1 . . . l, where do you go with that? Okay, yehh?? Yes there's more male pictures in the newspaper that are TOUGH, female pictures that are crying, you know, uhhh??" As long as teachers are not taught specifically how to teach about stereotypes and discrimination, many teachers will not risk their own uncertainties to engage their students in this uncharted terrain. If teacher education could specifically address theoretical and practical strategies of *how* to teach young children critical media literacy with social justice issues, then primary school teachers would feel more confident and better prepared to engage their students in these topics.

Ms. Rogers mentioned that the media literacy training has helped her teach more critically as she now moves beyond the textbook. She stated, "I think I present more of both sides of things, like Columbus Day, when we're doing why we have Columbus Day. So it's like I read the story, but then I also tell them about other people's opinion." Presenting various perspectives and analyzing messages for bias teaches textual analysis and issues of ideology. This is often difficult for critical educators because recognizing difference is not the same as valuing all ideas, especially when some are discriminatory or harmful. Ms. Rogers spoke about one student who told the class that his father doesn't like Black people. Ms. Rogers said, "It's amazing. You know some of the values the kids are taught at home and then sometimes they're not correct, I mean . . . they're prejudicial and the kids haven't seen the other side. So, when you present them with the other side, it kind of opens up the conversation. I don't know what they say to their parents when they come back, but it's good to do that."

Once teachers decide to teach critical social justice issues, primary sources can be a powerful tool for helping students empathize with the victims of injustice. First person accounts of injustice have a power and authenticity that can help students understand issues at a deeper and more empathetic level.

Third-grade teacher Mr. Baker told about an experience he had using primary sources: "I went to Manzanar[4] last summer and they had a packet. The main aspect of it was diaries, short diaries of individuals who were at Manzanar . . . We discussed what happened and some of the reasons behind the internment. And then I asked them some questions about them, some probing questions: Why do you think this happened? How do you think the people FELT who were there? You know, got them to start thinking a little bit. That was kind of OK. Until I had the kids actually open up and start *reading* what these people had written. Primary sources, and it was like three or four, five minutes into the work and suddenly I could FEEL, this undercurrent in the classroom and I heard one of the kids say, 'Is this what this person really said?' I said, YESSS. And suddenly everybody understood it from a different level, what we were talking about and then we were able to have a discussion, you know: Well how does that compare to what's happening now? What do you think we would find in somebody's diary from Abu Ghraib? You know real heavy duty questions for fourth graders . . . I also had Teaching Tolerance from . . . the Southern Poverty Law Project and we're going to be doing some things with that and we'll be discussing them and obviously using the media literacy probing questions to get them to think about it some more." Many teachers don't teach social justice issues in their class because they don't know how to go about it. This teacher offers a useful example of how primary sources can be an excellent tool to help students develop deeper understandings of social justice issues and more empathy for the victims of discrimination and injustice. Primary sources that provide perspectives from people who have experienced marginalization or oppression work well within a framework of feminist standpoint theory.

Another strategy for teaching critical media literacy is using a Freirean problem-posing pedagogy. Mr. Baker did this when he posed the problem of Japanese internment to his students and then connected it to questions about current-day situations of social injustice. Mr. Harvey demonstrated this when he took his students on walking field trips around their neighborhood. He explained that while on the walking field trips "I wanted them to focus on their community. What did they see out there as problems. They came up with people throwing trash around, it's dirty, there's a lot of noise. Then I had them try to come up with solutions. What would you do to help or address some of these problems?" While this was an excellent beginning for critical media literacy, unfortunately he ended the activity with the discussion, and the students never had the opportunity to actually tackle some of the problems that they encountered. Critical media literacy can be an excellent opportunity for real action in which the students can become agents of change through creating alternative media, writing letters, photographing the situation, circulating petitions, or any type of action they believe will, in some way, counteract the problem they want to solve. Some of the actions that teachers mentioned taking include creating t-shirts with messages that address environmental issues, making animations to counteract problems of violence, drawing posters that offer different perspectives on urban wildlife, and producing a PowerPoint presentation to educate others about recycling and convince them not to pollute. Through taking action, as small as it may be, students have an opportunity to feel a sense of agency in the face of situations that can too often overwhelm them into apathy and depression.

New Obstacles

During the 2004–2005 school year at Leo Politi Elementary School, the Academic Performance Index (API) scores dropped in language arts from an API-2 to the lowest level, API-1. The school failed to meet its Average Yearly Progress (AYP) for target growth and was placed on a Watch List mandated by No Child Left Behind (NCLB). Once a school drops to API-1, the NCLB mandate allows a school only two consecutive years to improve or else fall under much stricter control from outside as it becomes a Program Improvement School. Since Leo Politi is now in its second consecutive year of possibly failing to meet the AYP target, the district has become more involved in the daily operations, as onsite visitations and observations from district personnel have increased. Resentment to the increased observations and an atmosphere of fear were echoed in many of the teacher interviews.

During the 2005–2006 school year, a new principal and assistant principal took over the administration and made many changes. They instituted what they call the "Daily Three," a focus on instruction in three main subjects: language arts, math, and English language development (ELD). They put all the classes on a daily schedule for when teachers have to teach each subject and required written lesson plans. They also closed the computer lab and began writing up teachers who were not planning or following the program. Most of the teachers interviewed cited these changes, or effects of these changes, as significant reasons for not teaching media literacy. When I mentioned this to the principal, he disagreed and said, "I think that can be used as an excuse, I think that they weren't maybe actually using that [media literacy] before, or that it stopped, or they were maybe using it when you were here but then over the course of time it stopped being used." He insisted that if teachers had felt that media literacy was something worthwhile and that they were no longer able to teach it, then they would have brought it up to him and they could have discussed it. However, since nobody ever mentioned this to him, he insisted that the teachers were using these changes as an excuse for not teaching media literacy.

Table 1 Leo Politi Elementary School Timeline

2001–2002	2002–2003	2003–2004	2004–2005	2005–2006
SMARTArt begins first year New principal	SMARTArt continues with second year API-2	SMARTArt continues and ends with third year. API-2. Modified consent decree New assistant principal	Test scores in language arts drop, making the school an API-1 Politi enters the Watch List	New principal and new assistant principal Observations intensify Second year API-1 Computer lab closed Focus on the Daily Three

When the SMARTArt teachers were asked what were the major impediments keeping them from teaching more media literacy during the grant, and today, almost all of them stated that the lack of time was the prime obstacle. Most said that during the grant, as limited as time was, they had more time available than they do now because of many changes at the school site. During the grant, SMARTArt teachers received permission from the superintendent of their local district to integrate media literacy with Open Court during language arts and also to use ELD time for media literacy. However, now at Leo Politi, all teachers are expected to use the *Into English* curriculum for teaching ELD.

Ms. Brown explained why Leo Politi is right now not a good place for media literacy: "At this moment, Politi is so concerned about being right on the tip of maybe being taken over, maybe becoming a school that someone is going to be here constantly monitoring us, that they are so crazed about that, that the focus is just language arts. Language arts and math, has become this miniscule little subject and by the time you're done with all this language arts and recess and lunch, you hardly have time for anything else." Ms. Hernandez complained about not enough time to teach media literacy and said that it is more difficult now because "we have the Daily Threes: Open Court, Math and ELD. And that's it. Whatever you can do with art or anything else, just plug it in somehow and make sure that you tell them why you're doing it. It's really strict now-a-days." She stressed the need to incorporate other things into the scripted curriculum. She stated that there are "just so many things that we have to add, the Open Court is good, but there's a lot of things missing from it."

Ms. Ramirez said, "The other day, [Ms. Rogers] and I were sharing how the [media literacy] core concepts were so important for the kids, if we only had time to just teach it longer and be part of the school day because the kids do come out of there being more aware of all the different little elements, whether it's violence, just being aware that, oh, that's just sensationalized, it's not true. There's somebody that's going to come by and pick up the person that's dead out on the street, things like that. We shouldn't ignore it because children watch more TV now than they ever did before too, so just making them aware at an early age and then progressively teaching them the higher concepts or the deeper related concepts in the upper grades, but I do think it's important and we should incorporate it, but how do we do that? We don't have time."

When I asked Ms. Rogers why there is so little time, she blamed the rigidity of the OCR program and the new administration's focus on the school's low API scores. She said, "If we don't do something about it, we have threats of the State coming and taking over. So, we have a lot of administrators and coaches coming through, just on the spur of the moment, you have six or seven people walking through and they want you to be [on schedule], you submit your daily schedule so when they come, they want you on schedule. And for me, teaching . . . doesn't work on time limits like this, you have to kind of keep to those time limits, so that's kind of restricting and putting anything else in there than what they have given you. It's the Open Court and they're trying to match Open Court with ESL [English as a Second Language] class too, Into English, and so we have Open Court stories or units matched to our Into English and we're supposed to be doing our Into English, those particular units with our Open Court so it doesn't allow, that's when you can bring media literacy in, when you're doing ESL." When Ms. Rogers was reminded that using ELD time was how many people taught media literacy during the grant, she stated that "it's a little different now because of our situation. And they want to make sure everybody is teaching. They want us to use those units and we have unit tests that we put in from the Into English so it's gotten a little stricter." Since Ms. Rogers is an Arts Prototype teacher she still has artists coming into her class to work with her students during time set aside for art. While this could be an excellent time to teach media literacy, Ms. Rogers mentioned that that art time is "really very quick."

The ability of OCR to dominate the time in the school day and thereby the pedagogy and content of what can be taught and how was obvious when Ms. Rogers commented on the benefits of production. She said, "I think it's one of the greatest tools for teaching, to do some kind of production with it. It goes back to the same old thing of time, planning it and once you present it, it's wonderful, but it's just the time, the planning and integrating it because Open Court has this script, strict script, rules and what you should do, what you should say, it's kind of hard to put in a lot of production and creativity. They say, you can do it, if you plan right. You can do it during, what they call, IWT, Independent Work Time. But IWT is maybe 30 minutes."

Since OCR is a program designed for children who speak only English, it is more difficult to teach it to students learning English as their second language. Ms. Rogers, like many teachers working with second language learners, usually uses IWT to help students with vocabulary and issues that OCR does not address for kids learning English as a second language. Ms. Rogers stated, "Talking about a regular, on level, second grade class, I think you could put media literacy in very well because the kids wouldn't take as much time with this Open Court, but for the kids who are learning English and doing Open Court, it takes more time, you have to find more opportunities to present Open Court in different ways so that they understand it. So all that time, you're presenting Open Court, but in different ways so they can understand the concepts of Open Court. But, I think in a regular high-functioning English level classroom, you could do Open Court and present it the way they have it in the book and it would go as quickly as they say it would in the book and then you'd have time to integrate more things from other areas into it. But, when we integrate things into it, it's dealing with the words, the vocabulary that they use so we go download pictures from the computer or the internet and either bring in pictures so they can actually see 'lurking,' words like this."

Assistant principal Mr. Hudson insisted that the teachers have a regular time slot of 45 min at the end of each day for doing any lesson they would like. He insisted that this block labeled Mixing Time could be ideal for teaching media literacy. However, this is the only time available for teaching social studies, science, technology, visual and performing arts, and physical education. Even though OCR integrates some of these other curricular areas into its language arts instruction, there is still very little time for a teacher to bring his or her personal interests or other lessons into the classroom. Patricia Crawford (2004) documented a case in which commercially packaged scripted curriculum, like OCR, contributed to a lowering of teacher standards and a redefinition of teaching as a technical skill of implementation rather than a creative constructive process. She reports that teacher deskilling "is manifested over time in the lives and work of teachers who must navigate highly-scripted cur-ricula and who encounter technical control on a daily basis" (Crawford, 2004, p. 209).

Mr. Ruiz explained that now that the grant is over he would like to use photography and other media to teach language arts, but doesn't. "I think it's really just a time issue. They walk through the classrooms, we get a visit almost every other day. If they walk in and see the kids taking pictures, this adminis-tration, I think they'd understand what I'm doing, but the other big hot shots coming through would be, 'No, no, no. I think you need to follow the plan and there's no get the kids cameras and go take pictures.' They're worried about how we're putting things up on the wall or if a table is too close to the connect-ing door. They're writing people up for having stuff up on the wall too long." Mr. Ruiz commented on the obstacles that exist today at Politi: "Time and the pacing, the way it has to be, now we have strict guidelines on schedules and les-son plan books. They're basically telling us what to put in the lesson plan book and at what time and how much time is dedicated to it. It doesn't exactly run the class for you. But there is part of me that I'm worried that they're going to walk in right when, where we may be doing some art or more hands-on activi-ties, but it's just time and schedule and the way OCR is run and ELD."

Mr. Gomez stated that now he is using very little of what he learned from the grant because of the requirement to "follow the script. You have to follow the Open Court script. What I think may happen is that if I'm doing a lesson on media literacy, per se, they might say, 'Well what is that? Where is that in the Open Court curriculum? What section of the Open Court book is that?'" When asked what would happen if he were to tell them that what he was teaching is in the state standards, he said, "They might say, 'is it in the manual, is it in the guide?' If I have to say, 'no,' then they'd say, 'no you can't do that.' It could be held against me. Because I've heard that they ask you, like, if a teacher was doing something that's related to what's being taught, but was not Open Court and they asked him, 'What are you doing? What is that?' and he had to explain himself."

I asked Mr. Gomez if it is not enough just following state standards? He replied, no, "they say, 'Open Court is based on the State Standards, so do what they say and you'll cover the standards. That's proven. Your doing your own thing is you doing your own thing.' That's what they may say, but to be honest, I haven't done a lot of, barely any of the media literacy stuff, but that's what could happen to me if I tried that. Like, if they come in here, and I did what we did before, the video of the Star Wars and the viewpoint, the evil look in cinematography, they might say, 'What are you doing?' 'I'm teaching viewpoints.' 'That's not in the Open Court scripting.' That's what I suspect. And I don't want to get on their bad side because we get along well." Perhaps Mr. Gomez is using this as an excuse not to teach media literacy, as the principal suggested, or perhaps not. When I asked assistant principal Mr. Hudson about teachers using other material instead of OCR or Into English to teach the same standards, he said that teachers may "supplement but not supplant" the purchased curriculum. While that response might sound succinct, it is not a simple distinction when time is so limited. Often, supplemental activities make it very difficult to stay on schedule without something having to give. While integrating media literacy with language arts was one of the goals of Project SMARTArt, including new concepts within a highly structured and paced regiment can be a huge challenge. The administrator's assumption that one can supplement without supplanting lacks the flexibility necessary to integrate new ideas with confidence and support. The distinction between supplement-ing and supplanting can be highly subjective, and within an atmosphere of fear, many teachers will not take the risk that by modifying a lesson, someone might write them up for going too far off the script.

The largest chunk of school time is now spent with OCR, and the new pressures keep Ms. Rogers intimidated from going off the pacing plan. She stated, "they walk through so often. You don't want to have to go through explaining why you're doing this." She comments that they were visiting her twice a week and writing down copious notes while observing. She states, "at one time, six people came into my room. Six people! And, you know, it's kind of hard to carry on a lesson when there are this many people, what are they doing, they were just writing notes about you, what you have up and then you wonder why do they keep coming, what's wrong. They haven't given us any feedback and that was one of the things that was brought up at the faculty meeting. If you're going to come in, then tell us why you're coming and what's going on. If you want, you can ask, but they won't tell us."

As the pattern of fear and intimidation kept surfacing from the teacher interviews, a follow-up interview was conducted with one of the most expe-rienced and respected teachers of the group. Ms. Martin has taught for many years and holds an advanced degree in education. I asked her if she thinks that teachers at Politi feel scared or intimidated to teach only what is explicitly mandated and not other items they believe are important such as media lit-eracy. She said, "The fact that I even doubt myself doing it is important. I'm a veteran teacher. I am educated, I have a degree and I don't get accosted, I don't get harassed at all. I feel so much the opposite, but I live in that fear because I don't know. I talked with another friend of mine . . . we don't know when we're, when it's going to be us. You just don't know and this is totally anonymous right? [I reassured her, "absolutely."] My gosh how scary, I'm even afraid this is going to get around. It is crazy. I don't know if this is benefiting the children in any way. Well, what I think it is, is it's making people want to leave. I want to leave. This is completely anonymous but I want to leave. I want to leave the school that I have invested so much time in, that I love and I even feel supported but I don't like this, I don't like it." While the random observations may be intended to improve bad teaching, they are also creating a climate of fear where even good teachers feel intimidated. Michel Foucault explains that an effect of Bentham's panopticon was that it controlled the prisoners without the need for material constraints or physical violence. Foucault writes, "Just a gaze. An inspecting gaze, a gaze which each individual under its weight will end by interiorising to the point that he is his own overseer, each individual thus exercising this surveillance over, and against, himself" (1980, p. 155). The gaze at Leo Politi Elementary School is not a friendly glance, and as Ms. Martin's reaction clearly shows, it is taking away the essential qualities teachers need to make education come alive; they need trust, respect, and support.

Mr. Gomez expressed the same fear as Ms. Martin. He mentioned that he gets observed once or twice every 2 weeks, and those unannounced visitations intimidate him to follow the scripted program. He said that he "is not able to fully implement the media literacy lesson because I'm afraid they might not approve of that." He also mentioned that the lack of support and resources for technology have hampered his teaching media literacy.

During 2 years of the grant, Mr. Gomez was one of the most technologically savvy SMARTArt teachers, who would often use his laptop computer and LCD projector as well as movies they had seen before to make "connections to real life." When asked if he was still using computers and technology like he was before, he answered, "Not as much because I don't have a good overhead projector. They have one of them they put in the computer lab and the other one they keep for the office, for office presentations so I have to go ask for it. Plus, my Internet connection is down here, the wireless isn't working right now. They took one base out and the only one that's available is in the Teachers' Lounge. So from here, all the way to the teachers' lounge I have to try to connect and these white boards are magnetized, so it blocks it even further. On top of that, the signal is being broadcast but the internet connection is not being sent through. So it shows, oh yeh, I'm connected to the airport, but it says, not connected to the Internet. Obstacles. There's no one in charge of the computer lab. There isn't support for the hardware and stuff like that. There's no one in charge. The computer lab has been shut down. They only have someone helping with computers and trouble shooting, like four hours on Mondays. That's it. So I told them, this Internet connection is out. I told them a week and a half ago. I might have to go there myself, but I don't want to do that, I have so many things to do."

Assistant principal Mr. Hudson gave two reasons for why the computer lab was closed down. He said the computer lab closed "because it is not being properly utilized in the sense that, in the past, Leo Politi used to have a computer lab teacher. When the kids get into the classroom there'd be carefully planned instruction delivered to the kids. And right now we don't have a teacher in the computer lab and the principal felt that there was no set curriculum, carefully planned curriculum for utilizing the lab. And he doesn't want to use it as just a situation whereby people go in there to waste time. So he said until we'll be able to have a committee to sit down and come up with a program that's beneficial, that will support what we are doing in the classroom, that the computer lab will remain closed. That's one reason . . . another reason why it's closed down is most of the computers in the lab are obsolete, they are not working well because they are old. So he said that in most cases that you go in there to use the lab and you run into so many obstacles in the process, you waste a lot of time, not accomplishing anything."

Mr. Harvey, who used to work as the Leo Politi computer lab teacher, responded to me about Mr. Hudson's justification for closing the lab. Mr. Harvey asserted, "Those computers are not obsolete. Yes, they are six years old, but they are good enough for our students. The problem is that they don't have anybody to support the hardware and software integration. But he is right about no plan on how to use it. They need a teacher, but since OCR came out, all of the focus is on that. This problem is district wide at the elementary level especially. There are very few out of the classroom positions in the computer lab any more." David Buckingham (2000) writes, "Investing in the technological infrastructures—'wiring up' schools, for example—is a merely cosmetic gesture if it is not sustained by an investment in specialist staff and in training" (p. 203). The current policies for educational use of technology from the federal government on down through the state, county, city, district, and to the individual schools all reflect more of a window-dressing approach than a real commitment to the literacy needs of the students. Funding is occasionally invested in hardware but rarely in training or support for using the technology.

The choice of prioritizing the Daily Three at the expense of technology reflects a limited perspective on what is and is not language arts, ELD, and math. The effects of these choices reach beyond the computer lab right into the classrooms. Ms. Rogers commented that she has only two computers in her classroom that work and "we don't have people to service them, so if they're broken in your classroom, they're just broken. If you find somebody that knows about computers and ask them to come over if they have time, but there is no one really to service the computers." The absence of a person available who can troubleshoot technology problems onsite creates a barrier for any teacher interested in integrating into their curriculum multimedia tools such as computers, digital cameras, DVD camcorders, LCD projectors, and sometimes even TV and VCRs.

In spite of all the recent obstacles at Leo Politi, it is not the present school site administrators who are being blamed for the changes by most of the teachers. Some teachers believe that the current principal is, in fact, more supportive than the last administration during the grant. Mr. Baker stated, "Previously, we had administration that was not terribly supportive of it. He appeared to be supportive, but wasn't . . . I think that if we had the administration we have now, when we had the grant in place, things would have gone so much differently. Administration makes a world of difference." Another teacher echoed the same complaint about the previous administration. Ms. Brown commented about one year during the grant when "there were so many administrative issues that should never have occurred and they were just really based on the office not doing what they needed to do. It was really hard when somebody like [the dance teacher] came and the auditorium was taken for something else. Those are real obstacles because they really infringed on someone. Even [the music teacher] having to be in a classroom with music. There was someone next door to him trying to teach. I think that was a big part of it, it was just the administration was not supportive."

Ms. Jones stated, "I know that there was support to some degree among the hierarchy of our school, the principal liked having the idea that it was in the school, but it wasn't something that he was saying, well, now everybody is going to have this much time in a week or a month because we have to do what we have to do . . . all the tests for Open Court and all the tests for Math, so it seems like I felt, not oppressed quite, but near it, because there wasn't any time for creativity with what we were doing."

Mr. Baker complained about the lack of time to teach everything but used that problem to explain his strategy of integrating media literacy. He stated, "I've learned that really the only way that I can do it is to have it integrated within what I'm doing already because there's no time otherwise. No time." He integrates media literacy into language arts during OCR as well as social studies. Mr. Baker commented, "I talked about the Open Court instruction. I also try to incorporate it into the other curriculum as well, to social studies. When we get back on track, we're going to talk about the Gold Rush and we're going to talk about why, what role did media play in having a gold rush take place? Why did they do that? What was their purpose? Get them to understand the Gold Rush, for example, much better than they might otherwise. It's basically just to ask, I think probably, for me, the best and easiest way is to try to, anytime we have any kind of communication in the curriculum, be it through a story, be it through an article, be it through whatever we're doing, ask some of those media literacy questions. The Core Questions and get them to think a little deeper on what they're doing."

Ms. Martin commented that in spite of the fact that she is a veteran teacher, she is still being impacted "because there's so much to teach and trying to get in everything with media literacy, I have to integrate and it takes a little bit more creative thinking. And I can do it and I do it, but not to the depth that I would like to. If I had more hours in the day, if I didn't have to teach . . . but my kids get other stuff, they get music, they get dance, because that's important. So, it's harder. Maybe I just need to be more open, I don't know. But, yes, I can see where the scriptedness of it [Open Court] and because it's so assessment-driven, that many teachers probably would say, 'forget it, I'm not going to do it at all.' That makes sense. You have to do what you have to do. I think you can do it, you just have to really think about it, maybe talk with people and figure out ways. So that you can do media literacy and everything, you just have to for the kids."

One former SMARTArt teacher who now works as a coordinator at a different school in the same district lets on that the changes at Politi are not limited to Leo Politi. Mr. Harvey spoke about his new school: "even though the principal hasn't said you can't do that, it's the overwhelming pressure from above. The testing, the testing mania, all that stuff. The pressure to use Open Court and the Math Program." He states that teachers are supposed to use the purchased curriculum, and if they don't, they "may be subjected to some criticism."

New Barriers for Special Education

Another recent change affected special education especially hard. In 2003, the Los Angeles Unified School District (LAUSD) Modified Consent Decree (MCD)[5] required compliance with 18 different outcomes, one being the placement of special education students in regular education classes. An effect of the MCD is that the classrooms that used to have the most flexibility to implement media literacy now have the least possibilities of integrating it into the curriculum since most of the day the special education students are dispersed to numerous classrooms and the special education teacher has less consistency and time than before.

For the first 2 years of the grant, all the participating classrooms created their own animations with the help of the AnimAction artists on the day of production. During the third year of the grant, SMARTArt funding purchased the technology and training necessary to create animation without the AnimAction team. However, the only teacher (with the exception of an after-school paraprofessional) who managed for her students to create an entire animation on their own was special education teacher Ms. Brown. She explained how her class was the only one to complete an animation on their own, "I think that's partly because I have a small class and I have a wonderful assistant and between the two of us and some of the kids who have done it in the past, we were just able to get something done and we gave up other things where I think general ed couldn't. Our time wasn't as watched as it is now and I was able to keep my kids all day. So let's say, we finished Math and we had a half hour, we could get something done. My assistant, since I have a full time assistant, he could call over one child to do the coloring or something. It wasn't necessarily the perfect way to get it done, but it did show us that it is possible to get it done. But, this year, there is just no way. We just can't."

When Ms. Brown was asked if she is using what she learned from the media literacy grant, she said, "Quite honestly, this year, no. I haven't because my students leave, I have my second graders leave by 10 A.M. and my third graders leave by 8:15 and then I'm left with my fifth graders. I don't have any fourth graders this year. My fifth graders stay with me until 9:10. In that time, I pre-teach or post-teach the Open Court lesson we had prior and then once we leave at 9:10, none of us come back until 1:00. So when we come back at 1:00, and we don't always all come back at 1:00 because sometimes the third grade teacher keeps his kids a little longer. He has them come back after lunch. So, really, all we have left is an hour and 24 minutes and that's basically, math. It's the first time, since the morning, that we're back together as a class." Ms. Brown explained that the reason for these drastic changes at Leo Politi is because of the way that the MCD is being implemented.

Ms. Smith stated that media literacy has not been happening much in her class either because "we have so much going on with our language skills in here and now that most of the kids are all mainstreamed into different classrooms, it's something that has been like the first semester, it's just been a lot of preparing them to be more comfortable speaking." She mentioned other issues of mobility, self-esteem, and language as priorities to work with her students on since now they are leaving her class so much. Ms. Smith said that the biggest obstacle keeping her from teaching media literacy is the requirement to send all of her students out of the room. Ms. Smith stated, "Yes, so you're sending them out, you're having to be aware of when they go out and what's best for them, then they come back and they now have an issue." Managing students as they come and go, as well as all the new issues they bring back with them, keeps Ms. Smith too busy to bring in additional concepts, like media literacy.

Two special education teachers have left Leo Politi and are currently working as resource specialists at other schools. Since they no longer have their own classes, they have less freedom and are seldom in a position to be able to introduce new concepts like media literacy. Mr. Shaw stated, "in Algebra right now, which is the main subject area that I teach, there's not a whole lot of room for it [media literacy]. I don't do a whole lot of planning. I go in there and change or accommodate the students, what is expected of them, so I'm in there for them to demonstrate other ways, demonstrate mastery in other ways." Mr. Shaw also mentioned that he is very limited by the lack of time and a large number of students he is expected to service. He reported that the main obstacles keeping him from teaching media literacy are subject matter (algebra) and the structure of his job. Mr. Shaw said, "I provide a recurring service for kids who need a bridge from the gap of not understanding to understanding and that's where my focus is. My focus is not to teach them new concepts, it's to teach them concepts they've already been presented with and explain it in a different way so they can understand. And that's the biggest [obstacle to teaching media literacy]. I don't have my own classroom. I can't teach the kids what I want or what I think they should have, so I'm at the mercy of other people." The other special education teacher, who is no longer at Politi and has become a resource teacher, is Ms. Hendrix. She commented, "it's difficult for me to plan that intensively because I'm moving from K–5 and from room to room and kid to kid and people are all over the place in different parts of the pacing plan, so that's a little difficult. So it's really more orally that I make media literacy connections. It has to be an oral discussion to access the connections that they make, to their surroundings, to their immediate surroundings to media at large, etc. So, that's what I am doing and I think that's a limited view and attempt."

Ms. Brown commented that now "with No Child Left Behind, the push is so severe on my students to produce and it's like punishing them for being special as opposed to embracing them and trying to help them. I think that was maybe one of the nicest things about this [grant], that they were just so able to be accepted for who they were and they were able to shine and maybe not in ways that you could test. I know we tried a few times to figure out ways to test them. Maybe that was hard for them and I know some of them spoke to you privately and maybe it didn't always come across, but they really did, they learned so much and me too."

Recommendations for Making Media Literacy Flourish

The previous tendencies that were culled from the interviews reflect the teachers' beliefs in the importance of media literacy, different approaches to media literacy, and reasons why most are not teaching media literacy now. In the final section of this chapter, we hear from the teachers about what they believe would help make media literacy not only a seed of change that could grow, but a plant that could flourish. Most of the teachers felt strongly that media literacy should continue, and the following are suggestions they offered for how to best make it happen.

One piece of advice that almost all the teachers mentioned was the need for support from top to bottom, but not as a hierarchical imposition. Many wished for the possibility of having once again the support they had during the grant, while most wanted even more support from within, rather than just from outside the school.

The most common suggestion from the teachers was for more time and support for them to collaborate on planning and teaching media literacy. While reflecting on her experience during 2 years of the grant, Ms. Vargas said, "I just wish I would have had more time to plan and maybe even plan collaboratively with other media literacy teachers. Even though we weren't all on the same grade level, some of the concepts, hearing from different grade levels how they're going to teach a certain concept, all I would have to do is modify it for my students. I don't want to say that there weren't any opportunities, I just wish there were more opportunities."

Mr. Gomez emphasized the importance of sharing and collaborating among teachers. He suggested the ideal would be weekly meetings "to discuss what activities we had done related to media literacy. Then you get to share with each other and the other person reminds you, gives examples of what you can do, and at the same time, it helps you review what needs to be done and just keep going like that. That's what I would imagine. I do know when teachers come together and they share their ideas, other teachers say, oh that's true and they think of other things, it sparks creativity." The power of collaboration and the importance of using language as a tool for collective problem solving can benefit both teachers and students. Neil Mercer (2007) uses an example of three people working on a crossword puzzle to demonstrate how using language to collaborate can solve problems that none would be capable of solving alone. Mercer writes, "Information is shared, but more than that is achieved. Using the tool of language, the three people together transform the given information into new understanding. As a result of their combined intellectual efforts, they solve the problem" (p. 2).

Ms. Martin spoke about needing the support of peers like she had during the grant. She said, "one thing that I feel that I'm missing is a group of people. I think that would really help. I don't know if there's a way to create a study group of people who are interested in media literacy or even just constructivist teaching in general, social justice, just so that we can continue the conversation. That would help. I think about how I learn and if I have books and we're talking about the same thing and are on the same page and when we were part of the media literacy training, it helped to be with other people and to have all this training because you were in the middle of it. When you leave it, it's so hard to get back into it."

Another aspect of collaboration that was mentioned by Ms. Ramirez is peer teaching. She told about an experience she had during the grant that required her to share some media literacy lessons with the other second-grade teachers during a grade-level meeting. She said, "I felt really successful then because I was talking to my peers and they understood what I was saying and it just seemed like the lessons went very smoothly. I didn't have to stop and explain. They knew what we were doing and I saw it being done in other classrooms and I think that's why I felt so successful. I felt like, oh, that's so cool."

Mr. Gomez stated, "Teachers need reminders, I guess just refreshers, on the concepts of media literacy and how to go about it. I think so much has been coming down from the district and all that, that it's all about Open Court, it's all about Reading, Writing, English Language Development stuff and so I think we kind of forget about other things that can be taught, like media literacy and things like that . . . Opportunities to review what you know. Because that's what they're doing with us with Open Court and math with the coaches, they're constantly reminding us, this is how you go about doing things and giving workshops to support it and trying to take us to another level. They keep us going that way, which is good. It reminds you how this needs to be done and let's keep that going."

Mr. Gomez mentioned the value in having a media literacy coach "going around saying, do you need help with something, you know, support. A teacher may say, 'well I'm having a little trouble with this.' 'Well, let me see what you do. Maybe we can tweak it this way,' stuff like that." He said, "That's where the ideas about different viewpoints of the animals and all that came about. Having the time, making the time to plan for it with other people who are like-minded individuals, as they say. But it is a challenge. When we signed up, we made an agreement that we would be doing this, so we were kind of obligated, we did say we're going to do it. Once that obligation is done, it's easy to just kind of continue focusing on what we did before."

Ms. Vargas also felt that a media literacy coach is very important to provide feedback. She said, "now that I'm a [Open Court literacy] coach, I think about how I've seen teachers, their practices improving, maybe their pacing improving because I was there to help and give feedback." She spoke about the value of having a media literacy coach to observe lessons and provide feedback about "if my questioning was on target, or if I would have added this question, it really would have gotten me to where I wanted the children to be."

The need for ongoing support was echoed by many teachers. Mr. Harvey stated that just the learning process alone requires lots of time. He said, "it took at least two years, the third year, we were just starting to roll; we started to internalize it. When you internalize it, then you can look for places." Like Mr. Harvey, Ms. Vargas also mentioned feeling overwhelmed by the difficulty of trying to learn media literacy and then also trying to teach it at the same time. She said that she wishes she had more time "for myself to really let it absorb so that then I can, in turn, give it to the kids. But, I think for me that was one of the most important media literacy moments, just like being conscious of my own learning. I just wish that I would have gotten to the point where I was handing it off to the kids a little faster."

Could the teachers' call for support back the principal's remark that the teachers are using the new changes as an excuse not to teach media literacy? Once the grant ended, all of the support also ended. However, to say that the implementation of a strict pacing plan, a schedule of what to teach when, and a new climate of fear and intimidation are merely excuses is far too simplistic. Two years after the grant ended, at Leo Politi there is no support, and on top of that, there are new rules that make teaching media literacy even more difficult. The complexity of the entire situation in context reveals many more causes to explain why teachers are doing what they are doing. If anything, this is even more proof of the need for some type of mandate and funding to support systematic implementation of media literacy that will include collaboration, ongoing trainings, coaching, peer teaching, and feedback as necessary elements for media literacy to flourish.

Ms. Ramirez frames media literacy as a useful tool for teaching language arts and ELD but complains about the lack of structure and support for teaching it. Ms. Ramirez stated, "Even if media literacy became an English program, I just thought that the amount of time, the realia that we had was rich and it was authentic. It wasn't something that we were trying to pull out. I just felt that for me, I needed more structure in order to be able to be more effective. I felt like I was always second guessing myself, which might be another obstacle because I know we fed off of other people's ideas, but there really wasn't, to me, I never felt like there was a concrete guideline, you have to do this, you have to do that, everything. It's great to have options cause everything was optional, to do this, but I feel the children might have gotten more out of it if I would have had even more structure and even more follow-up. Sometimes I would do a lesson on Monday and I couldn't follow it up until Thursday, in an English [language development] program, I think it would fit the best."

At the end of the first year of the grant, several teachers worked together and created introductory media literacy lessons and two lists of vocabulary words, one for lower grades and one for upper elementary.[6] This, combined with the CML's five core concepts and key questions, were the primary tools and framework for SMARTArt teachers. Ms. Vargas commented on the importance of having a common language and framework. She stated, "I think the first thing is just getting all the teachers on the same page as to the terminology and the core concepts of media literacy, just the language that's involved in the curriculum of media literacy, like sexy kind of advertisements and the whole gamut." She stressed the importance of this because, "if teachers are really comfortable with language and comfortable talking about media literacy, then they'll be more comfortable to just embed that."

Mr. Gomez liked the idea of having a packet of specific media literacy lessons like the introductory lessons the first year teachers created. He stated, "I remember that it was something to start off with. That would be good for teachers who want to introduce something to the students. I don't think it'll replace, but it helped jump start some kind of media literacy. Here's the packet, introduce it because the teachers will get it as they teach the lessons. It's the kids that need the support. The teachers, if they read it, they can kind of understand, oh, this is what it is basically."

Mr. Ruiz and Ms. Ramirez spoke about the value in backward planning (Wiggins & McTighe, 2001). Mr. Ruiz stated that the best way for kids to learn is "if you backward plan and use more of a whole language approach." Backward planning requires the teacher and students begin by understanding the goal and purpose of the lesson. Mr. Ruiz said, "if the goal is to get the kids to understand multisyllabic words, then using newspapers, using and finding, just backward planning using these lessons. The kids won't even realize it's media literacy, it's that a specific media literacy lesson, they can hear it in music, they can hear, they can use their ears to listen and pull out words from music. Backward planning I think might work."

A distinction needs to be made between simply free exploration and a structured program that creates opportunities for directed exploration that can lead to deeper levels of awareness and discovery. Ms. Ramirez commented, "Back then [about a decade ago with Whole Language] it was more about having the kids experience and having them come up with, what are we learning and why are we learning it? That was back then. That was when we were doing that whole, oh, you have to have children make these realizations on their own, which is part of team teaching, which I don't mind, I think it's great. But, I think some things need to be explicitly told to the kids. I don't think that kids would have understood what I was trying to do. Maybe because I never had taught it before, but I don't know, for me, it felt like it was the right thing to do. 'Guys, we're going to learn about this because of this.'" Backward planning offers many positive metacognitive benefits that empower students to become more aware and more in control of their own learning.

Ms. Jones suggested that the best way to integrate media literacy into the elementary school curriculum is doing it "their way" and scaffolding the concepts by grade level. By that she meant you need a "reason for it. So, it would be fine if we weren't presented all the facts at the same time. Maybe starting in kindergarten where they're concentrating on some of the basic facts, like color and maybe emotions they can understand and become more sophisticated. After, those in first grade could pick-up and add to that. I think that would help students pick it up faster if they had a background instead of all at once." Ms. Jones offered these ideas as a constructivist vision for teaching media literacy systematically across all grade levels. She also asserted the need for teachers to be part of this process, "It would be nice if teachers could have something to say about that and I know we started putting lesson plans in folders which students lost or disappeared, but if a few on grade level decided among yourselves to be responsible for creating a couple of lessons and you held on to them at grade level, I think that would work. Put some of the goals that they keep saying, they have to be able to write paragraphs, they have to be able to do this and that, I think they could do that over, by looking through some of the curriculum guides that they already have, some of the standards we have to meet."

A previous teaching method at LAUSD involved teaching content connected through thematic units. Now with scripted skills-based programs like OCR, lessons might be thematically grouped but teachers are not encouraged to design units around themes. Ms. Jones commented that even though it is "not in fashion right now," thematic teaching might be an easier way to teach media literacy. She said, "I think one way to get away with that is in the primary grades, where you can push your specific ideas so they can really be mastering something in media literacy that goes with their theme. But when you get to the more sophisticated, where you want them to come back with critical thinking, they've had more background." Ms. Rogers liked some aspects of OCR but thought that combining thematic teaching with the phonetic parts of OCR could work well. She said, "I think more than integration and not being so rigid with the schedule and it's like the teacher's creativity, is not there, so I think a mixture of both could be possible."

Mr. Shaw also spoke about the value of thematic teaching for integrating media literacy into the elementary school curriculum. He said, "I guess the best way is to start with a theme and that theme can then harbor within or engender, expand upon the critical questions, the essential questions. Without a theme, you lose focus and the questions become entities that are disconnected. There needs to be a focal point. I think that thematic based teaching is the way those questions need to be brought into the elementary school." He suggested beginning by explicitly teaching media literacy vocabulary and the key questions. "Then I would take a theme and I would say, now we're going to apply this in a concrete way, and apply the questions to a theme, throughout that unit," said Mr. Shaw.

Often, thematic teaching is done through projects, sometimes referred to as project-based learning. This is another strategy that was mentioned for teaching media literacy and making learning more experiential. Many best practices for teaching (Zemelman, Daniels & Hyde, 1993) include both thematic and project-based pedagogies. Ms. Jones told about a project her fourth-grade students undertook that flowed naturally from an OCR story and addressed a real problem that her students recognized and wanted to solve. After reading about middle school boys who started their own business, Ms. Jones had her students create their own products that they could sell. This assignment required that students plan everything from focus groups for assessing needs to advertising campaigns for selling their products. Working in groups they discussed media literacy concepts and explored issues of gender and target audience. When Ms. Jones's students encountered a real problem that existed at their school, they focused their project to solve it. They discussed the fact that many students are dropped off at school at 6:00 A.M. and are not picked up until 6:00 P.M., when their parents finish working. Waiting for 2 hr before school was boring and Ms. Jones's students decided to create board games that would be academic and fun for the students who have to arrive early and have nothing to do. The process of making real products that had value to others taught her students many lessons and gave them a strong sense of pride. Ms. Jones said, the games were such a success that other students also began making their own board games, "it had a little life of its own."

The notion that media literacy should involve production as well as analysis has become a widely accepted tenet of media literacy movement proponents in the U.S. The benefits of media production are numerous, especially when creating media is part of project-based learning. All the teachers interviewed agreed that production can improve learning for many reasons, from being more motivating to making learning more intrinsic. Ms. Hernandez asserted that when students do something and not just talk about it, "the benefit is that they'll take it with them for the rest of their lives." Ms. Ramirez commented that when learning is hands-on, "I think they solidify their learning much quicker and are able to express themselves a lot clearer." Ms. Martin spoke about an activity where her students photographed adults on campus for a newspaper they created. She said, "They started to notice things when we looked at newspapers because they had done it themselves. And I think critically, they were able to look at media in a way they hadn't looked at it before."

Mr. Baker said that when children create, "they learn so much deeper . . . because it's a multi-modality, they're using different parts of their brain, different aspects of their personality, different aspects of things they have learned. To be able to express something using different media, they are using different parts of their brain and they're trying things together." Mr. Gomez commented on the value of production as a means of authentic assessment. He said, "If they're able to do that project, then they're starting to internalize what they're learning, hopefully, and if they get it, they'll produce a product that reflects the learning. So if they get the idea, of any concept you're trying to teach, and they're able to produce a product that reflects what you're trying to teach them, then it's proof that they understand it."

Production offers the benefit of letting children have first hand experiences, and experiential education is something that Mr. Shaw recommends to his students. He said, "I always tell the kids I work with, in order to learn a concept, three things need to occur: you need to see it, you need to say it or hear it, and you need to do it. So, that was the doing part." This recommendation is similar to Fredric Jones's *Positive Classroom Discipline*. Jones insists that students need to be doing more and listening passively less (Charles, 2002, p. 57).

For Project SMARTArt, many different media projects were created from plays to posters and from newspapers to animation. Yet, of all the projects and products, the main culminating activity was the animation, something many of the teachers spoke about as being their most successful moment. Unfortunately, the animation screenings for parents during the first year of the grant had very few attendees. Ms. Vargas remarked about the importance of having some type of culminating activity or event such as "a media literacy night where they're sharing, or maybe presenting, things to each other."

Ms. Jones commented on the need to involve parents more in media literacy, since they were interested but often didn't know what their children were doing or why they were watching TV as homework. She said, "I had parents ask me once in a while at a [parent] conference or when they saw me in the yard, what is this stuff they're doing at home for media literacy? Because sometimes there would be a question left over from presentations that they had to think about in their journal and have it out, write it or talk about it at home. The parents weren't quite sure what we were doing. They knew we weren't brainwashing them to think a certain way. They knew they were supposed to be looking at a lot of media and bring in things from magazines and newspapers. They weren't quite sure why." During the grant, this was an area of concern for many teachers, and two workshops for parents were taught in the evenings to attempt to address this need. Ms. Jones's comments about the need for including parents in media literacy education reflects a weakness of Project SMARTArt and an important recommendation for future media literacy work.

Several teachers mentioned the need to apply media literacy ideas to technology and use more computers. Ms. Jones asked, "I just wanted to know if these projects couldn't be incorporated more into computer projects? So you can make DVDs, at least by the time you get to middle school or high school. If this is a project that's going through the grades, if we set them up to do everything basically by hand so they see the process, maybe by the end of fifth grade they ought to be doing a project that's computer driven." It was mentioned to her that many media education researchers are pushing for embedding media literacy in the new computer literacy (Luke, 2004). She commented, "I think that's a good place for it because that and the amount of time students spend on computers doing things that they don't really need to be doing, when they're out of school, if they had something that was interesting to do that they learned at school, maybe they would become more creative again instead of just passive."

Ms. Vargas is one of two SMARTArt teachers who have left the classroom to train other teachers as literacy coaches. Her advice for teaching teachers about media literacy follows an experiential model where teachers learn through doing. She stated, "I go through that learning experience and then think about what was it in the presenter's strategies or methods of presenting this to me that helped me understand it and how I can thereby replicate that with my own kids at an appropriate level so that they can feel successful learning it the way I just did at the end of this PD [professional development]. It's a different kind of PD, it's not like I'm presenting a concept and let's plan it, it's like I'm making you go through the experience so that then you can replicate it with your own students. I think that would be valuable." This type of hands-on learning is part of the pedagogy that was promoted in the SMARTArt trainings and follows an experiential process that is useful for children as well as teachers (Dewey, 1916/1997).

Few teachers offered specific suggestions for what administrators can do to make media literacy flourish. Most mentioned the need for support, something that could easily fall to the jurisdiction of administrators. However, the current administrators know very little about media literacy, and according to the new principal, no teacher has yet spoken to him about it. It seems that most teachers view administrators more as managers of a bureaucratic system than as agents of change who could encourage innovation and transform policies. Mr. Baker commented in general about what a good administrator should do. He said, "For one thing, they can do what we were trying to do and that is encourage more people to become involved and when they do get involved, support them." While this remark about support is quite broad, the experiences that he and other teachers encountered during the grant were often reflective of insufficient quality and quantity of backing from their administrators. Mr. Baker and Ms. Smith also spoke about the need to help students have more of a leadership role and voice in the school. They both suggested student media production, such as a school newspaper, as a possible path to this goal.

When Ms. Hernandez was asked about what suggestions she had for implementing media literacy, she responded enthusiastically, "try to bring it back somehow." She stated that for this to happen the teachers would need somebody to set up "more time for us to do it and creating more enthusiasm because I think we've lost it. We kind of lost it. OK, we don't have to do it, that kind of a thing. Maybe if you could create more enthusiasm with the administration, they're very good, they're a good group of people that love instruction and that's what they're here for, to make us work. But, I love it, I think if you could create enthusiasm in them, that would be great." Ms. Hernandez makes an important point about the value of not merely support, but enthusiasm. The infectiousness of enthusiasm should not be undervalued as an important aspect of any new program. While true enthusiasm cannot be required, buy in and ownership are important motivating qualities for teachers and students.

Conclusion

The interviews with these 14 Project SMARTArt teachers are not intended to provide conclusive proof that media literacy does or does not work. They are not a quantifiable set of data that generate numbers and charts to prove or disprove effectiveness, if that were even possible. However, they are something else very important; they are qualitative evidence from experts in the trenches, teaching in an elementary school and attempting to implement some of the theoretical ideas that are discussed throughout this book. These are voices seldom consulted or listened to when theory is developed and policies are mandated. Yet, the insights learned from practical daily applications can be profound and much can be gained from these interviews.

These teachers reflected upon and shared their ideas about *why* and *how* to best teach media literacy. They espoused their beliefs about the importance media literacy holds for their students. Through discussing their ideas about media education, they help compare and contrast the differences between art education, media literacy education, and critical media literacy. They recounted experiences with obstacles that interfere with all their best intentions to teach media literacy in their classes. They brought to light the importance of media education for special education students as well as new obstacles for these same students. Finally, they have provided a plethora of recommendations for how media literacy can best be taught in elementary school. Although the majority of this book explores theoretical ideas, these voices offer a powerful resource to balance theory with practice in order to inform each other and benefit both.

In the first section of this chapter, the teachers discuss the importance of media literacy. They offer a large list of benefits. Mr. Baker positioned media literacy as an essential building block for literacy education and asserted the importance of teaching students when they are young that all messages have a purpose. Several teachers suggested that media literacy is an important metacognitive skill to help students think about thinking. They also mentioned that media literacy helps students think "outside of the box," a most important skill for creativity, innovation, and transformation. Mr. Ruiz provided a wonderful example of critical autonomy (Masterman, 1994) when his students flipped over their new book covers in a move to resist the co-optation from the advertisers who donated the book covers to promote a movie. This simple act of resistance reflected independent critical thinking and student empowerment to challenge stealth advertising that slipped into the school cloaked as charity. Mr. Shaw mentioned the possibility that these new skills can help students see differently and with more empathy. The ability to "step into other people's shoes," as Mr. Shaw mentioned, is an important part of critical media literacy and standpoint theory. It is this type of understanding that can lead media education toward the goal of critical solidarity (Ferguson, 2001).

Throughout the interviews many different benefits of media literacy were mentioned, including building awareness of media and advertising, teaching about different points of view, and using the inquiry process to explore and pose critical questions. Several teachers mentioned the importance for them personally of learning this new information about mass media and popular culture. Ms. Jones commented on the changing media culture the kids are growing up in and the need for schools to help this new generation "start learning something about it." This idea about the disconnect between schools and our mediated society is an important reason for expanding the concept of literacy and bringing media literacy into the classroom (Buckingham, 2003).

Issues of developmental appropriateness generated some interesting differences between a couple of teachers. Though all the teachers agreed that media literacy should be taught to children at all ages, two teachers argued against pushing social justice issues in the early grades. Mr. Harvey and Ms. Ramirez both believed that many sensitive issues such as homophobia, racism, or sexism are inappropriate to teach in the lower primary grades. During their interviews, this resistance seemed based largely on their fears of not knowing *how* to teach controversial topics to young students. This issue of what is and is not developmentally appropriate is difficult to discuss in the abstract since each class and each child is unique and the context of all these issues is so dynamic that they are always changing, as are the children and the problems. Through answering these questions, teachers provided comments that reflect some of the fears and concerns they carry about engaging with social justice issues. For the majority of the teachers interviewed, these topics were embraced and addressed with less apprehension and more as issues that they would address in their classes as they arise. Ms. Rogers spoke about dealing with racism with her second graders when one student voiced his father's dislike of blacks. Only a couple teachers actually used a problem-posing pedagogy where they brought these problems to their students, such as Mr. Baker's use of primary sources to teach about Manzanar and then connect that injustice with current issues such as prison abuse at Abu Ghraib.

Unfortunately, only two of the teachers interviewed, Ms. Smith and Mr. Shaw, worked with any students younger than second grade, and they both taught special education with multigraded classes. Both spoke about the need to engage students of all ages where they are at and with whatever issues that arise from the students. The absence of kindergarten and first-grade teachers from the data sample is an unfortunate weakness of this research. In the next chapter, this issue is discussed further through the analysis of two teachers' work with preschool, kindergarten, and first-grade students.

The inclusion of special education classes in Project SMARTArt and four of those teachers in this data sample has been very fortunate. Through analyzing the interviews with Ms. Smith, Ms. Brown, Ms. Hendrix, and Mr. Shaw, it became apparent that media literacy holds considerable potential for special education students. These teachers reflected on the marginalization of special education that often occurs in public education and the importance of making media education available to their students as well as to general education students. These four teachers spoke about the benefits media literacy offers their kids through lowering the affective filters that often interfere with student learning. The multimodal quality of media education allows more avenues for students with all sorts of needs and abilities to participate at different levels and in different ways. Ms. Hendrix spoke of the importance of bringing critical thinking lessons to her students, and Ms. Smith mentioned the value of having her students address issues of representation since they are so often misrepresented or underrepresented in the media. Issues of representation are so intimately linked with self-image and identity that exploring these concerns with special education students holds great potential for them personally as well as academically.

Even though all teachers agreed on the need for media literacy, various types of media education were discussed. When analyzed within Kellner's four categories, it is impressive that none of the teachers embodied a protectionist approach. Since protectionism is basically a negative perception of media and a limited pedagogy for students, this absence reflects a positive feature of how the teachers think about media and their students. The most common approach to media literacy expressed by the 14 teachers interviewed is the mainstream notion about media literacy in the U.S. This media literacy movement approach embraces many important concepts of cultural studies that are necessary for critical media literacy to be taught later. Since the grant was structured as an integration of art education with media literacy, many teachers were very comfortable with the art education approach, yet often pushing it to be more critical and inclusive of cultural studies concepts. Ms. Rogers's comments about wanting her current Arts Prototype teacher to be more critical seems to reflect an understanding of the limits of art education and the potential that media literacy offers to make up for those gaps. Since the training that all the SMARTArt teachers received emphasized integrating media literacy as much as possible, it is not surprising to hear so many of the teachers discussing this as their primary strategy for teaching media literacy. Integrating media literacy into their curriculum is also one of the best approaches to solve the problem of insufficient time to teach everything. Several teachers spoke about the need to incorporate media literacy into their instruction as the only way to find time for it. One of the ways they mentioned incorporating it involves expanding literacy to include popular culture like t-shirts and magazine subscription cards. Another aspect that was mentioned was simply applying the CML key questions to any of their lessons.

Only a few teachers expressed specific critical media literacy concerns with issues of social justice. Ms. Vargas mentioned the value media literacy offers as a bridge for connecting social studies content with current-day issues. This is exactly what a couple of teachers did with lessons from the 1960s civil rights movement. Media literacy became a tool and motivator for bringing more perspectives into the classroom. Mr. Baker demonstrated an excellent use of primary sources with his unit on the Japanese internment camps in California. However, some teachers expressed resistance to engaging with social justice issues based mostly on their apprehension about how to teach such sensitive subjects. Mr. Harvey articulated this hesitation when explaining that he could teach some of these ideas but felt uncomfortable about where to take the lesson once the social injustice was exposed. This is where the focus of critical media literacy can offer important transformative pedagogy for empowering students through action-based projects that could involve numerous alternatives from creating counter-hegemonic media to writing letters. A Freirean approach to critical media literacy is a dialogical problem-posing pedagogy that seeks to turn students into subjects empowered to act on the world they are living in and learning about. These progressive ideas offer a powerful road map to answer Mr. Harvey's question about where to go. While the roadblocks and obstacles along this path are many, it is important to remember that the journey or the process is usually more important than the final destination or product.

Since the grant ended in July 2004, many changes have occurred at Leo Politi Elementary School. The standardized test scores dropped in language arts, thereby lowering the school's API score to the lowest level, API-1. Once this occurred, a new administration replaced the previous one and the district placed the school on a Watch List. The new administration, which began this school year, created a focus on just three core academic subjects that are tested with standardized assessment. They call this focus the Daily Three, and it is accompanied by a schedule for what and when all teachers are expected to teach every day. The administration required lesson plans to be submitted in advance; they closed the computer lab and have been writing-up teachers for being out of compliance. According to the teachers interviewed, many of the new changes have made teaching media literacy much more difficult. In an interview with the new principal, he rejected this comment by the teachers as merely an excuse. It is interesting to note the new principal's resistance to consider how these changes could have such consequences. The principal's comment echoes the current neoliberal agenda and NCLB's emphasis on accountability without support. The mandated schedule for when each subject must be taught aims for consistency and standardization throughout the school and across the district. NCLB encourages this push for efficiency and standardization, much along a business model. While a business model might function well for corporations aiming to maximize profits, standardizing children is not the best way to encourage participative democracy nor creative innovation.

Among the obstacles that the teachers mentioned, the biggest was the lack of time to teach everything they are expected to teach. This was also a problem during the grant, yet all the teachers agreed that it is even more difficult now. Most of the teachers felt intimidated to not rock the boat by an atmosphere of fear that was not present during the grant. Since the API level dropped, the school has received many more observations by district personnel than previously. These unannounced visitations of as many as six people at one time have had an intimidating effect on many teachers. Although none of the teachers interviewed mentioned being written-up themselves, many spoke about the fear of being written-up for not being on schedule or for doing something different, such as media literacy. Principal Sullivan said that he has already written-up between 6 and 10 teachers and some several times. Even assuming that only incompetent teachers are being punished for bad teaching, the interviews reflect an atmosphere of fear in which many first-rate teachers feel intimidated. The principal insisted that he is open and could give some "wiggle room," but since no teacher has approached him about teaching media literacy, he assumes that media literacy is something they really don't want to teach. Based on the comments from the interviews, it seems more probable that the structure of rigid schedules, scripted curriculum, and consequences for those who do not do as told are keeping teachers from doing many things they would like to do. The teachers also emphasized the importance of support that encourages innovation, which is the opposite of this climate of fear. Yet, in spite of this difference of opinion, none of the teachers interviewed blamed the new administration for these changes; most see it as consequences of NCLB and their school district's policies.

The other obstacle that several teachers mentioned is the closing of the computer lab. This is related to the school's focus on the Daily Three and the desire for constant accountability. The administrators claim to have closed the lab because of lack of a plan for how to use it and because they believe most of the computers are "obsolete." Mr. Harvey, who used to work in the lab, counters that the computers are old but not obsolete. He agrees that the computer lab was not being used systematically since there was no teacher running it, something he said is all too common throughout the district. However, instead of hiring someone skilled to run the lab, the administration took the easiest action, thereby removing one more tool from the teachers' and students' limited chest of resources. This is almost ironic since the administration is claiming to give top priority to literacy taught during the Daily Three, yet technology is not seen as part of that literacy.

While all teachers have to deal with these new changes at Politi, the special education teachers have yet another obstacle to confront, the MCD. The implementation of this decree at Leo Politi requires that all special education students spend the majority of their time in regular education classes. This may have positive benefits for special education students as they are mainstreamed into the general population. However, the special education teachers at Leo Politi have commented that they are now less able to teach media literacy since they are sending their students out to other teachers throughout the day. During the grant, special education classrooms had the greatest flexibility to teach media literacy; now they have the least.

In the final section of this chapter, teachers made recommendations about how to make media literacy flourish. The most common suggestion is for support, from the top down as well as horizontally, as teachers would like to work with fellow teachers to collaborate and support each other's efforts. Some teachers mentioned the potential of having a media literacy coach on campus, much in the same way they currently have two literacy coaches onsite. Ms. Vargas, who is now one of the literacy coaches at Politi, stressed the need for giving teachers feedback. Some teachers asked for more structure and media literacy lessons. This could be seen as ironic since so many teachers were complaining about too much structure from the scripted curriculum they are required to implement. Or, this could also be seen as an effect of a dependence on prepackaged curriculum that some teachers have become used to. However, since everyone is different, it makes sense that some teachers will thrive with more structure and others with less. An important point is that by making more media literacy lessons and structure available, those teachers who need that will have more resources from which they can choose.

Nobody commented about the need for more money or tools, such as digital cameras or computers. Most of the suggestions involved concerns about how to teach and suggestions for a progressive pedagogy reflecting many of John Dewey's ideas about experience and learning. A couple teachers suggested backward planning as a way to help students better understand the purpose of the lessons. Ms. Jones pushed for constructivist scaffolding of media literacy concepts throughout the grades as a way for implementing it more systematically. Teaching methods such as thematic instruction and project-based learning were recommended by several teachers. This advice also follows research in best practices that assert the value of learning by doing and linking learning through themes (Zemelman et al., 1993).

A few other suggestions involved the need for more parental involvement, more integration with technology, and experiential professional development to help teachers discover the value of media literacy. While all the teachers wanted more time and more support, very few suggested that administrators have a role to play in making this happen. The impact of federal, state, and district mandates seems to be disempowering teachers. The need for progressive educational reform that can counteract the myopic back to basics movement and the obsession with high-stakes standardized tests is essential if media literacy is to have the potential to become a truly transformative pedagogy.

This research has provided the opportunity to investigate some of the impact of a 3-year federal grant to teach media literacy and the arts at an inner-city elementary school and the current obstacles that some public school teachers face. Through listening to teachers who have been trained in media literacy and have had experience teaching it in elementary school, many lessons can be learned about the intersection of theory and practice. In spite of the obstacles and lack of support, all the teachers interviewed are strong proponents of media literacy for young children. They have also brought to light a seldom researched topic, that of the added importance media literacy holds for special education students.

Since most of the writing on media literacy focuses on middle school and high school students, these teachers' ideas and experiences can be helpful to other educators trying to learn what media literacy can look like at the elementary school level. The fact that most of the teachers interviewed are now teaching very little media literacy is a significant finding. This lack of continuity by the majority of the teachers suggests that media literacy needs consistent support and must be integrated into the curriculum in a systematic manner. The fact that much more media literacy was being taught while the school was receiving the federal grant demonstrates the importance of having a mandate to teach it and the funding to support it. Of all the suggestions the teachers offered, the most recurring comment was about the need for ongoing support.

CHAPTER FIVE

The Earlier the Better

Expanding and Deepening Literacy with Young Children

Most children born in the U.S. in this millennium have never known a time without the Internet, cellular phones, or television.[1] Practically every U.S. household has at least one television set and about one-third of young children live in homes where the TV is on "always" or "most of the time" (Rideout, Vandewater & Wartella, 2003, p. 4). Before most children are 6 years of age, they spend about 2 hr per day with screen media,[2] something that doubles by age 8, and before they are 18 they spend approximately 6½ hr daily with all types of media (Rideout, Roberts, & Foehr, 2005).[3] It is also estimated that nearly all young children in the U.S. "have products—clothes, toys, and the like—based on characters from TV shows or movies" (Rideout et al., 2003, p. 4). The implications for the amount of media enveloping today's youth is significant when one considers current research about literacy acquisition that suggests "the early childhood years—from birth through age eight—are the most important period for literacy development" (International Reading Association & National Association for the Education of Young Children, 1998, p. 1).

Technological innovations, expansion of global media empires, and unrestricted commercial targeting of children have all contributed to an environment where today's kids are growing up in a mediated world far different than any previous generation. While the technological advancements have created new possibilities for the free flow of information, social networking, and global activism, there is also the potential for corporations or governments to restrict the flow of information and appropriate these new tools for profit and control at the expense of free expression and democracy. Now more than ever, young children need to learn how to critically question the messages that surround them and how to use the vast array of new tools available to express their own ideas and concerns. Since television programs, video games, computers, cell phones, music, and even toys have become our current transmitters of culture, tellers as well as sellers of the stories of our time, it has become an imperative to teach critical media literacy to children as young as possible. Numerous examples and analyses of media education with college students and teenagers are now available, but very little has been written about critical media literacy with young children in preschool, kindergarten, and first grade. It is with these young children, between the ages of 3 and 7, that this chapter explores the possibilities of critically analyzing and creating alternative messages.

As described in the previous chapters, critical media literacy is a pedagogical approach that promotes the use of diverse types of media and ICT (from crayons to Webcams) to question the roles of media in society and the multiple meanings of the form and content of all types of messages (Kellner & Share, 2007). Analysis of media content is combined with inquiry into the medium, the codes and conventions, the media industries, and the sociocultural contexts within which capitalism and media function to shape identities and empower and disempower individuals and groups. This approach is hermeneutical and skills based; critical media literacy pedagogy integrates production activities with the process of critical inquiry. The potential of critical analysis increases when questioning is conducted through production activities that encourage students to examine, create, and disseminate their own alternative images, sounds, and thoughts (Share & Thoman, 2007).

Critical media literacy offers the potential for young children to develop multiple literacies, engage with popular culture, media, and new ICTs in ways that are meaningful to them, experience the excitement of creating their own messages in many formats, and participate as productive citizens empowered to confront their problems and transform society. Critical media literacy involves a progressive pedagogy that combines an expanded notion of literacy (including all types of media, technology, popular culture, advertising, as well as print) with a deep analysis of communication (exploring the relationships between media and audiences, information, and power). Issues of race, class, gender, and power can be addressed through a multiperspectival approach that integrates ideas from cultural studies, critical pedagogy, and media literacy (Kellner, 1995). Following Paulo Freire's (1970) *problem-posing pedagogy*, critical media literacy involves praxis, reflection, and action to transform society.

Often, false assumptions about children, society, and media keep many educators from exploring this new pedagogy. Popular ideas about what is and is not appropriate often prevent the possibility of discovering the potential of critical media literacy to engage young children in meaningful learning that develops their cognitive, social, emotional, moral, and political abilities. A large number of U.S. educators carry positivistic views of childhood that focus myopically on biology at the expense of considering sociocultural and political contexts (Steinberg & Kincheloe, 2004). Many educators consider teaching a neutral and unproblematic activity, something Henry Giroux asserts is based upon an instrumental ideology that is tied to the culture of positivism and "the various modes of technocratic rationality that underlie most school practices" (2001, p. 209). Kathy Hall (1998) warns that this perspective is not actually apolitical as is claimed, and instead "many practicing teachers' political naiveté concerning literacy, teaching and schooling, serves to perpetuate the status quo" (p. 187). Howard Zinn calls this common confusion the *myth of objectivity* and insists that "[o]ur values should determine the *questions* we ask in scholarly inquiry, but not the answers" (1990, p. 10).

Critical media literacy challenges a positivist conception of children as voiceless passive entities that need to be controlled and regulated by adults. Instead, Shirley Steinberg and Joe Kincheloe suggest, we need a view of children that embraces "the child as an active agent capable of contributing to the construction of his or her own subjectivity" (2004, p. 7). Understanding children as active co-constructors of meaning helps teachers guide students to ask deeper questions about information and its relationship with power, as well as teach students how to critique, analyze, and express their own ideas in multiple formats. Hall writes, "even quite young children can understand matters of equity, including matters like, say, sexist language practices and discriminatory social organisation. Young children's sense of fairness is usually acute" (1998, p. 187). Determining what is appropriate education for young children is a complex task that requires understanding cognitive abilities, considering social and cultural contexts, and scaffolding teaching to meet individual needs and differences. Barbara Nicoll states, "Teachers who use developmentally appropriate practices are doing more to promote critical thinking than traditional teachers who believe children are too young to think well" (1996, p. 2). Examples provided in this chapter demonstrate that critical media literacy can be taught to young children.

In today's mass-mediated culture in which young children need skills for interacting with new media and technologies, educators should be considering which sensorimotor and cognitive abilities will be most needed and what are the best developmentally appropriate practices for facilitating their growth. This is especially important when literacy is understood as a social, as well as a developmental, process of assimilation and accommodation. Rogoff and Morelli write that the role of "social interaction provides an essential context for development itself" (1989, p. 346). Marsha Kinder states, "Piaget claims that 'in order to know objects, the subject must act upon them, and therefore transform them'; in turn, the subject is transformed, in a constant process of 're-equilibration'" (1991, p. 4). As an example, Kinder asserts that video games "not only accelerate cognitive development but at the same time encourage an early accommodation to consumerist values and masculine dominance" (p. 119).

Victoria Carrington (2005) writes that the emergence of new media texts "situate contemporary children in global flows of consumption, identity and information in ways unheard of in earlier generations" (p. 22). A half century ago, Raymond Williams wrote that the effects of television are less about discrete items and more about a *flow* of programming running day and night. Tania Modleski describes Williams's concept of flow as the complex interactions and interrelations between various television programs and commercials (1982, p. 100). According to Alan O'Connor, a critical point of Williams's analysis is the notion that the flow of television is constructed to prepare viewers for advertising and it is "mainly irresponsible" (2006, p. 47). Beverle Houston explains, "The flow of American television goes on for twenty-four hours a day, which is crucial in producing the idea that the text issues from an endless supply that is sourceless, natural, inexhaustible, and coextensive with psychological reality itself" (1984, p. 82). She goes on to argue that this flow is one of desire and consumption in which the structured interruptions only enhance the desire for endless consumption.

Much of commercial children's television programming has advertising breaks every 5–10 min. During a typical half-hour show on *Cartoon Network*, a child watches about 20 commercials. This advertising often uses the same cartoon characters from the program that she or he is watching (*Scooby Doo* hawking *Gogurts*) or movies (*The Simpsons* toys at *Burger King*) and other popular culture to sell products. These crossovers and merchandising relationships are examples of what Kinder refers to as *transmedia intertextuality*. Kinder writes that Saturday morning television and "home video games, and their intertextual connections with movies, commercials, and toys, help prepare young players for full participation in this new age of interactive multimedia—specifically, by linking interactivity with consumerism" (1991, p. 6). However, this is no longer just Saturday morning cartoons; the flow is now constant with *Nickelodeon*, *Cartoon Network*, *Disney Channel*, and the Internet (that now offers programming and accompanying games); children's television is available all the time, for those who can afford it.

Children's transmedia intertextuality reaches from the bedroom to cyberspace, as everything from cartoons to junk food is available 24/7, with games to play and merchandise to buy. Children have become a multibillion dollar consumer market that are bought and sold, observed and analyzed by some of the largest corporations in the world (Buckingham, 2000; Kanner, 2006). Merchandising and mass marketing construct a flow that links everything together: television, movies, music, Internet, toys, food, clothing, and sometimes even school. The system functions so well that it often goes unnoticed as a natural part of the cultural environment. This normalization veils the historical construction and corporate planning of highly sophisticated marketing strategies and techniques targeted at children. While this may seem commonplace today, it is important to remember that advertising to children is a relatively new concept. Jyotsna Kapur points out that "[i]n the early 1900s, there was a certain embarrassment in profiting off childhood" (1999, p. 128).

Ideas of media flow and transmedia intertextuality supplement Horace Newcomb's and Paul Hirsch's notion of television as a cultural ritual. Newcomb and Hirsch (1994) write that television functions as a cultural ritual and "ritual must be seen as a process rather than as a product" (p. 505). They focus on the cultural role of entertainment and TV as they quote James Carey about the ritual view of communication that is directed toward "the maintenance of society in time; not the act of imparting information but the representation of shared beliefs" (1983, p. 504). Herbert Marcuse (1991) and other theorists from the Frankfurt School (Horkheimer & Adorno, 2002) stress that while media are imparting information, they are also perpetuating ideologies, shaping epistemologies, and socializing consumers. The common experiences children have with their media encounters at home are then acted out and shared in schools and playgrounds, and interconnect with other media texts in the private and public spheres. By contextualizing media as a cultural ritual, the focus moves away from a specific television program or episode to focus on media as a whole system, the flow, the viewing strip as text. This notion of media as ritual and flow offers a larger contextual framework for analysis to situate media in relation to other social influences such as parents, schools, government, church, and the like. A broader vision can also reveal the manner in which media *position* audiences. Using this "culturalist" approach, Buckingham suggests:

> Rather than attempting to measure the effectiveness of news in communicating political information, we should be asking how it enables viewers to construct and define their relationship with the public sphere. How do news programmes "position" viewers in relation to the social order—for example, in relation to the sources of power in society, or in relation to particular social groupings? How do they enable viewers to conceive of the relations between the "personal" and the "political"? How do they invite viewers to make sense of the wider national and international arena, and to make connections with their own direct experience? How, ultimately, do they establish what it *means* to be a "citizen"? (2000, p. 175)

It is also important to consider the political economy and ways that power and ideology are used by corporate producers of children's media culture. Steinberg and Kincheloe (2004) assert that children today are growing up in a *kinderculture*, a consumer culture dictated by corporate concerns for profit. They write, "Since the 1950s more and more of our children's experiences are produced by corporations—not parents or even children themselves" (2004, p. 30). Kincheloe states, this kinderculture has rerouted children's cultural identification and affect, "working twenty-four hours a day to colonize all dimensions of lived experience" (2004, p. 131).

These changes in society and media require a paradigm shift in education from a purely cognitive psychological model to one in which psychology embraces sociology in the understanding of literacy as a social process embedded in the contexts of history, politics, economics, culture, and power (Luke & Freebody, 1997). While children are growing, their cognitive abilities are not isolated from their social and moral development; therefore literacy should be taught as a social process in which critical questioning becomes a regular strategy for engaging with all texts, as early as possible.

Another factor that often prevents educators and parents from engaging young children in questioning and creating media is an excessively protectionist attitude toward young children and media that overvalues the power of media and undervalues children's abilities. As mentioned in Chapter Two, media educators who embody this protectionist model do not provide their students with a critical or empowering pedagogical experience.

The point is not that media have no effects and that children are all powerful and should be allowed to view any media any time. Media representations can have direct effects causing nightmares, anxiety, and even trauma when children are exposed to images and/or content that are too scary or disturbing for them. All children have the right to live free of fear and violence and they need to be protected from dangerous influences, both in fiction and in nonfiction. Some media experiences are more pernicious to children when encountered in nonfiction, such as news programs, than when viewed in fictional entertainment (Buckingham, 2000, p. 136).

However, most media effects are indirect and long term (such as reinforcing male privilege within a patriarchal society or contributing to eating disorders in a culture obsessed with body image), repeated as transmedia intertextual flows that permeate society in the information age. This process cannot be censored; the best protection we can provide children is education that will empower them with *critical autonomy*[4] (Masterman, 1994) and prepare them to participate as active citizens in *critical solidarity*[5] (Ferguson, 2001) with the world around them.

The Earlier the Better

While it is important to protect children from inappropriate experiences and representations, it is also important to understand that most children have the ability to begin questioning their media much earlier than often occurs. As demonstrated in the previous chapter, both students and teachers have the ability to understand many of these complex ideas when they are taught through active media production and developmentally appropriate analytical activities. Experiences with my own son have also demonstrated that from a very early age[6] some children can understand many basic media literacy concepts of media construction, multiple perspectives, and commercial motivations.

Young children not only have the ability, but for the sake of developing critical teenagers and active citizens, it is essential that we start as early as possible to plant these seeds of inquiry. Rather than denying young children opportunities to explore controversial ideas about media because of assumptions about children's inabilities and deficiencies or fears about the dangers of media, we should investigate *with* children the possibilities for connecting their personal experiences and concrete ideas with critical questioning about their lives and the mediated culture in which they are growing up.

Critical media literacy can also make abstract ideas more concrete when students create their own media and experience constructing their own representations. Learning through doing allows children to apply theoretical concepts through hands-on activities. When teachers create the space for students to experiment in multiple modalities with issues of representation, audience theory, political economy, and social justice, then students will be better prepared to understand these ideas in greater depth later. Teaching critical media literacy to young children is by no means an easy project, yet as you will see in the examples provided, it is feasible to teach many children much earlier than most adults realize.

Teaching critical media literacy requires epistemological movement in two directions: a horizontal expansion and a vertical deepening. The horizontal motion entails a broadening of the definition of literacy to include multiple ways people read and write, view and create information and messages. This expansive notion of literacy consists of serious study of popular culture, advertising, photographs, phones, movies, video games, Internet, and all sorts of hand-held devices, and ICTs, as well as print. Along with analysis, it involves production, as students learn to create messages with different media and technology. Many of these ideas can be found under various labels, such as multimedia literacy (Daley, 2003), new literacies (Kist, 2005), multimodal literacy (Kress, 2004), multiple literacies (Kellner, 1998), information literacy (American Library Association, 2006), technology literacy/computer literacy (Thomas & Knezek, 1995), and visual literacy (Debes, 1969).[7]

Some of the horizontal expansion of literacy also inclines to the vertical movement toward a sociological deepening that frames literacy as more than a purely cognitive thought process. Critical media literacy understands reading and writing as social practices embedded within social contexts. It is this sociocultural framing that requires vertical movement to deepen the questioning of the interconnections between information, knowledge, and power.

According to a definition created by a panel from the American Philosophical Association (Facione, 1990), *critical thinking* involves cognitive skills ("interpretation, analysis, evaluation, inference, explanation, and self-regulation") and affective dispositions ("a critical spirit, a probing inquisitiveness, a keenness of mind, a zealous dedication to reason, and a hunger or eagerness for reliable information"). This cognitive/affective definition provides an important part of understanding critical thinking; however, it lacks a sociological understanding of communication and information.

Meanings are not only created inside someone's head, but they are also always dependent on historical, social, political, economic, cultural, and numerous other contexts in which the text is created and in which the text is received. The social construction of knowledge makes it impossible for information to ever be neutral; it always connotes values and ideologies. In addition, the concept of an active audience suggests that individuals and groups of people negotiate meanings similarly or differently depending on the experiences, values, feelings, and many other influences that shape their group and individual identities. Adding this sociological understanding to a cognitive/affective definition of "critical thinking" opens up new possibilities to embrace the many social dimensions of how we think (Luke & Freebody, 1997).

The vertical movement in critical media literacy unites the skills and dispositions of critical thinking with a social consciousness and an understanding of knowledge as socially and historically constructed within hierarchal relationships of power. The rejection of the notion that education or information can be neutral and value free is essential for critical inquiry to address social injustice and inequality through transformative pedagogy based on praxis (reflection and action). Giroux writes, "Education is not training, and learning at its best is connected to the imperatives of social responsibility and political agency" (2001, p. xxiv). This type of pedagogy can be found under many labels, such as critical literacy (Luke & Freebody, 1997), critical pedagogy (Darder, Baltodano & Torres, 2003), critical reading (National Council of Teachers of English & IRA, 1996), and critical multiculturalism (Cortés, 2000).

For critical media literacy, the horizontal expansion of literacy and the vertical deepening of analysis are intrinsically connected, but for many educators they are often separated, as teachers working within one approach do not consider the need to link with the other. It is not uncommon that teachers doing excellent work in media production fail to engage their students in critical analysis of the very media they are creating. At the same time, many progressive educators have their students critically deconstruct the power relations in historical documents and books but fail to apply those same critical questions to popular culture, technology, or mass media. These myopic perspectives are even more shortsighted when working with young children because of the preconceived limitations that many educators have internalized.

Viewing these two educational approaches as separate can be helpful to understand their differences and similarities, but critical media literacy is built on the integration of multiple media and production with critical inquiry and social justice. To demonstrate the differences between the horizontal and the vertical movement, examples are provided from two teachers, each working primarily out of one of the two approaches. Both teachers demonstrate excellent models of developmentally appropriate teaching practices that are child centered, promote active learning, and encourage deep understanding (Geist & Baum, 2005). While the pedagogy of both teachers is first rate and does occasionally overlap the broadening of literacy with the deepening of critical inquiry, only occasionally do they unite the two ideas into a critical media literacy framework.

One of the easier routes for horizontally expanding literacy is available via ICTs and the current interest in technology literacy. Carmen Luke (2004) suggests that if media literacy can enter schools through "the 'backdoor' into computer literacy education," then it will have a better chance of being accepted. However, computer literacy is different from media literacy since the former is primarily a positivistic approach that appropriates new tools to unproblematically transmit content, while the latter requires problematizing media and technology to explore how the content and the audience are affected by the communication process. Recognizing the differences can help educators take advantage of the support and funding available for technology literacy to expand the notions of literacy on the path to critical media literacy.

Patty Anderson: Expanding Literacy

The first example comes from a public charter elementary school in the LAUSD in which the teacher, Patty Anderson, had the same students for kindergarten and first grade. Working with 20 bilingual children for 2 years, Anderson created a multimedia classroom that integrated technology and media into her core curriculum. For 2 years my son was a student in her class and I regularly observed and assisted the students and teacher.

Due largely to the conservative political climate and backed by requirements of the federal law, NCLB, the present expectations for early childhood education have become more academic and skills based. In LAUSD, like many other school districts in the U.S., the majority of kindergarten classrooms are now full-day and are expected to have students reading before first grade. This movement is also ratcheting up academic expectations for children between the ages of 3 and 5 as most states have now adopted early learning standards in literacy, language, and mathematics (Neuman & Roskos, 2005a). Even Head Start, the longest running federally funded school readiness program, has been legislated to ensure literacy growth with several goals, including letter recognition and phonemic awareness (Dickinson, 2002).[8] The focus on print literacy and phonics-based instruction has forced many kindergarten teachers to minimize art activities, playtime, and experiential learning for more standardized and often scripted phonics programs (Hemphill, 2006; Miller, 2005; Tyre, 2006). According to Susan Neuman and Kathleen Roskos, the skill and drill routine in early literacy instruction "may inevitably consign children to a narrow, limited view of reading that is antithetical to their long-term success not only in school but throughout their lifetime" (2005b, p. 2). They assert that reading achievement is less about sounds and letters and more about *meaning*. Neuman and Roskos write, "It is the higher order thinking skills, knowledge, and dispositional capabilities, encouraging children to question, discover, evaluate, and invent new ideas, that enable them to become successful readers" (2005b, p. 4). Since Anderson teaches at a charter school that runs a full bilingual program in Spanish and English, she has more flexibility and control over her curriculum than most teachers in her district who are required to follow the scripted phonics-based OCR program and the district pacing plan.

Anderson is a young teacher who enjoys using media and technology in her daily life and recognizes the importance of teaching her students to become technologically literate as early as possible. In kindergarten, Anderson began teaching her 4- and 5-year-old students how to take photographs and use photography to communicate. She comments, "I think a lot of us use pictures in our daily teaching, but I think it's more powerful to use pictures that the kids actually take." She explains how most kindergarten teachers she knows purchase commercial packets of photographs that illustrate specific themes or concepts, but through working with her students to create their own images, she finds that abstract ideas become more concrete and the students take more ownership of their learning.

Her students began kindergarten studying the theme of "caring," so Anderson had them discuss how they could visually show this idea. Once a student was able to act out caring, another student would photograph one moment that the class agreed conveyed the idea of caring. Using a digital camera, Anderson then downloaded the images that the children took and printed them out as minibooks with just the pictures and the title in Spanish, "cariño." Each child was able to take home their own book that same day to reinforce their learning and encourage a love of books. During math, Anderson had her students take the digital camera around the room and around the school to photograph all the different shapes they could find. By searching for shapes in their everyday environment through the lens of a camera, they were connecting math to their real world and seeing the familiar with a new set of eyes. These pictures were printed for the students to cut out and sort according to different attributes. The students' experiences with photography were also supported by minilessons about photography that I helped provide which can be found online at the CML Web site (Share, 2005).[9] Throughout the year of kindergarten and much more in first grade, the students were allowed to use the digital camera often as another instrument in their literacy tool kit.

Anderson teaches in a low socioeconomic area and has many students who begin their education in kindergarten, without any preschool experience. Therefore, one of her first goals in kindergarten was to teach the children how to recognize and form letters. One activity that supported this learning required the students lay down outside on the grass so that they could be photographed from above as they used their bodies to form different letter shapes. These photographs were displayed in the classroom and printed on homework pages as friendly graphic reminders. Along with the use of photography, Anderson utilized her own laptop computer and an LCD projector to demonstrate concepts visually whenever the lesson warranted it. Her school has a broad vision of literacy and the arts therefore all the students have an art and music teacher visiting their classrooms on a regular basis. During kindergarten, Anderson videotaped all her students for a movie they presented to the parents at the end of the year. This was something that in first grade, her students were able to play a much greater role in the production process.

In first grade, Anderson moved into a new room with her same students and with four computers. With the new technology, she was able to finally implement her desire to have her students create multimedia projects. During that year, I was able to volunteer a couple days each week and work with small groups of 4–8 children at a time. Most of the children had no experience with a computer and took considerable effort to learn the most basic concepts, like how to double click and drag and drop. Since the children were already familiar with photography and visual imagery, we began teaching them PowerPoint. We scaffolded the teaching of new computer skills incrementally: the first writing they did was with WordArt and then later they learned to insert a text box. Inserting pictures and animation was simple and fun so it made it easier for them to learn about folders and subfolders. As their skills progressed, the tasks became more sophisticated and the students began creating more computer projects that addressed the themes and content from their core curriculum. They used Microsoft Word for publishing their Writer's Workshop stories and PowerPoint for creating posters and presentations. The Internet was occasionally used with adult guidance, but the students were not permitted to surf the Web alone. Anderson's incorporation of ICTs into the core curriculum added to student's literacy development but did not replace other experiential and developmental activities, like drawing, painting, printing, acting, singing, discussing, experimenting, playing, and socializing.

While the school had a computer lab, other students rarely had the opportunities that Anderson's students had to use technology to communicate and create. This is in large part because of Anderson's philosophy that media and technology should be tools to empower students. Unfortunately, her school administration viewed media and technology as neutral conveyers of content for transmission, as opposed to teaching students to analyze these new tools and use them to create their own messages. At Anderson's school, most of the computers in the lab did not have a writing program but they all had a math game. While the kids loved to play it and the teachers saw their student's math skills and spatial reasoning improve, it would be a mistake to assume that this was computer literacy. Each child logged on to his or her own computer and for 30 min to an hour, he or she answered math questions with plenty of audio and visual stimulation. While students did indeed interact with this computer game, it was a closed type of interaction, one in which choices were limited by the few options provided. This contrasts greatly with Anderson's classroom where the projects that students created on the computers entailed much more open interactivity and student control as the children had many more choices about content and form.[10]

At the beginning of first grade, each student created a guidebook about another student, in which they had to photograph and interview a partner. Anderson gave each child a blank book in which to write about their colleague based on their interview, and attach the photographs to accompany the text. The 4–6-page books were shared with the whole class and swapped around during reading time. The series of photographs each student took of his or her partner were archived in all four classroom computers for use in other literacy and art projects. These archives grew as students photographed every field trip, guest speaker, and numerous class activities. They also began using the teacher's mini-DV camera to document their interests with sound and motion.

One of the obstacles keeping many teachers from even considering these types of activities is the fear that young children cannot be responsible with expensive equipment. Anderson states, "It's true that a lot of the fear I think that teachers have, that probably I had at the very beginning of kindergarten, is that they're going to ruin these things and that they're going to drop them or they're going to not be safe with them. But obviously, teaching them from the very early age how to handle that, then you get past that." Beginning in kindergarten, Anderson taught her students to always wear the strap around their neck and treat the camera as an important tool, not a toy. Since the technology has become so simple, no longer does the photographer have to set the light meter or even focus the lens. The old Kodak slogan, "You press the button and we do the rest" has been surpassed as now any child who can press a button can take a picture and see the results immediately. In the 21st century, any school or teacher that can afford a digital camera can easily make photography a valuable literacy tool for young children.

Throughout the 2 years, Anderson had her students create many projects, individually and collaboratively. The use of technology in the classroom was greatly facilitated by group work and peer teaching. A type of "interthinking" occurred as students collaboratively used language for thinking together to create media and solve problems (Mercer, 2007). The final culminating projects that Anderson's first graders produced included a movie about first grade and a PowerPoint show on endangered species. The purpose for their movie was to reflect on and document their learning and also to show new students what to expect when they begin first grade. Because of limited technology (only one camera and no editing software in the classroom), the students could not physically edit their movie. While they were able to film most of the scenes, narrate voiceovers, and discuss planning and editing choices, Anderson did most of the editing work herself.

For the final PowerPoint show, students were able to do all the production work themselves. They worked in pairs to create 4–8 slides about an endangered animal of their choosing. They researched about the animal from books and Web sites and then discussed why the animals are in danger of extinction and what they could do about that. They explored issues of global warming, habitat destruction, poaching, and contamination of the oceans and discussed ways they could help by minimizing pollution, encouraging their parents to drive less, and not dumping trash down drains that lead to the ocean.

Each pair inserted photographs, WordArt titles, and text boxes with information into their PowerPoint slides. Following the writing process, they wrote, shared, revised, edited, and published their work with the help of their partner and other students. The process required considerable work to make sure the photographs and the words worked well together, a literacy skill important for reading and writing. Anderson reflects on this process, "I hear them having this conversation about, 'well we shouldn't put a picture of an animal that's playing around when we're talking about something that's bad,' which I think is really good. And I've heard other pairs talk about the kind of pictures they want to include and where." After one pair discovered a mistake or something new, they would share it with others and before long everyone was making similar changes. The sense of ownership and exploration that students felt while working on this project led some to take the project beyond the teacher's expectations. On their own, one pair discovered symbols and inserted a red circle with a slash through it, and soon others began inserting different symbols to accompany their photos and text. Working with the music teacher, the students wrote their own song about protecting endangered animals and performed it for their parents.

Another important aspect of both culminating projects was that the students were creating their presentations for real audiences beyond the teacher. Performing their PowerPoint show to other students and their parents gave the first graders a strong sense of purpose for their work and genuine feedback.

By reading the text they had written in each PowerPoint slide, the students had the opportunity to read and present publicly to an audience, thus meeting several state standards for language arts. Creating and presenting projects for a real audience is one of Foxfire's[11] *Eleven Core Practices* and is an important element of good pedagogy because it motivates students and provides deeper learning opportunities that are less likely to arise otherwise. After presenting to a kindergarten class, Anderson's first graders returned to their classroom and debriefed the presentation. The students were disturbed by the reaction of the kindergarteners to a photograph in the show of a dead whale with red blood in the water. They discussed the picture further and talked about the reasons for the presentation and the seriousness of the topic. While some students expressed their dislike of the picture and felt it shouldn't be in the show, others discussed the importance of saving the animals and the need to have a serious photograph, like that one, to communicate to others that animals are dying. The discussion that evolved from a real audience response to their work and picture choices took these 6- and 7 year olds into an analysis of the power of visual imagery and the appropriateness of their choices for specific purposes and particular audiences. This inquiry linked their concerns and use of different media with much deeper theoretical concepts of semiotics, audience theory, and the politics of representation. Neuman and Roskos (2005b) state, "Literacy development is not just a matter of learning a set of technical skills. It is a purposeful activity involving children in ways of making, interpreting, and communicating meaning with written language" (p. 5). Anderson's students accomplished Neuman and Roskos's purposeful content-rich literacy description and bumped it to a higher level by expanding the notion of literacy beyond just written language.

While Anderson did not design her class around critical literacy principles, she did engage her students in many critical concepts through questioning, discussing, and taking action by creating their own media messages. The atmosphere of open inquiry that Anderson created encouraged the autonomy and curiosity necessary for the development of critical thinking. Nicoll (1996) asserts that "Critical thinking skills can only be taught in an environment that encourages the children to ask questions, to devise ways of answering those questions, to make decisions about how to proceed, and to evaluate the quality of their answers." Engaging with the students' popular culture and asking questions (such as who created the message, how, and why) encourages students to critically reflect on the media they use and the media they create. Anderson also used interactive journaling, where she could correspond one-on-one with students, to encourage critical reflection.

For young children, posing questions that aim to reveal the construction of media messages can help them start to think about media differently and consider different ways of knowing. While it is important not to negate children's media culture nor destroy the pleasures they get from it, the denaturalization of media is necessary for children to be able to ask different questions. For example, when a movie is considered just entertainment and not understood as a construction of reality, then the questions that one can ask tend to be limited to the content of the movie. Anderson mentions, "I think in this age group, they have a tendency to think they know the difference between fantasy and reality, but a lot of the times, they struggle with it, they really don't know what is true and what isn't true. In a movie like *Ice Age*, there are elements of it that are true, that are based on the fact that there was an ice age, but what about the animals and what is created and what isn't. I think we talked that day about, someone had to write the movie, someone had to animate it and draw the pictures, because of the cartoons, so we got into a conversation about that."

Many of the mandated standards that students are expected to learn in elementary school cover media literacy concepts such as the California State Content Standards for language arts that list kindergarten students "Distinguish fantasy from realistic text" and they "Identify types of everyday print materials (e.g., storybooks, poems, newspapers, signs, labels)."[12]

Anderson clearly demonstrated that integrating media literacy concepts and technology skills into a kindergarten and first-grade curriculum is not only feasible but can be highly successful. While she faced many obstacles in terms of limited resources and difficulty in negotiating time constraints, she managed to make the lessons developmentally appropriate for her students and provided numerous opportunities for them to communicate with different ICTs. The deficit thinking and protectionist fears that keep many administrators and educators from engaging young children in these types of activities are not helping the students. Administrators need to let go of these misconceptions and place their time and energy in training teachers (not only how to use the new tools but more importantly how to teach *with* them and *about* them), providing ongoing teacher support, purchasing and maintaining ICTs, and then allowing teachers and students to use these new tools as components of an integral literacy program. Educators, like administrators, also need to relinquish old fears and embrace these new tools and new pedagogies as exciting opportunities to link classroom learning to students' lived experiences and mediated lives. Technology must not replace drawing and other experiential activities; instead it should expand children's full capacities by providing more developmentally appropriate opportunities to communicate and create (Miller, 2005).

Anderson's engagement with media and technology expands her literacy pedagogy horizontally yet only occasionally deepens her teaching vertically into a more profound analysis and critical action. For this type of critical literacy and sometimes critical media literacy, Vivian Vasquez offers some excellent examples and advice.

Vivian Vasquez: Deepening Literacy

Vasquez is a teacher who has written methodically about her experiences teaching young children critical literacy. She builds her curriculum on social justice concerns with an affirmative approach that seeks to empower students to confront injustice. Vasquez asserts that critical work with students "does not necessarily involve taking a negative stance; rather, it means looking at an issue or topic in different ways, analyzing it, and hopefully being able to suggest possibilities for change or improvement" (2004, p. 30). In line with Paulo Freire's (1970) *problem-posing pedagogy* and Robert Ferguson's (1998, 2004) concept of *productive unease*,[13] Vasquez writes, "A critical perspective suggests that deliberate attempts to expose inequality in the classroom and society need to become part of our everyday classroom life" (p. xv).

Through posing critical questions, Vasquez aims to disrupt authorial power and problematize social situations. Exposing the social construction of information and knowledge is necessary to unveil power inequalities. Vasquez follows the theoretical work of Alan Luke and Peter Freebody (1999) in Australia, who developed the *Four Resources Model* promoting a sociological emphasis in literacy education. Vasquez writes:

> Luke and Freebody assert that reading should be seen as a nonneutral form of cultural practice, one that positions readers in advantageous and disadvantageous ways. They argue that readers need to be able to interrogate the assumptions and ideologies that are embedded in text as well as the assumptions that they, as sociocultural beings, bring to the text. This leads to asking questions such as, Whose voice is heard? Who is silenced? Whose reality is presented? Whose reality is ignored? Who is advantaged? Who is disadvantaged? These sorts of questions open spaces for analyzing the discourses or ways of being that maintain certain social practices over others. (2003, p. 15)

When a child raises a question about issues that are unfair or unjust, Vasquez explains that a teacher has basically three ways to respond. The teacher can take a traditional *banking* (Freire, 1970) educational approach by treating the student's question as a fact, thereby positioning the teacher as expert and the student as a passive recipient of a seemingly "objective" factual answer. This response often ends the child's inquiry and curiosity with the false notion that information is neutral and memorization is the goal. A more constructivist teacher can turn the question back to the student and ask her or him what she or he thinks. This was a common response that Anderson used to encourage her students to be more independent and reflective. While reposing a question can be a useful strategy to stimulate cognitive critical thinking, it does little to transform the problem or the student. The critical response that Vasquez uses moves the student further toward empowerment as she challenges her students to collaboratively take action by asking them: "What can we do to change the situation?" (2004, p. 98). Encouraging students to take action is an essential component of transformative pedagogy and a necessary element of critical media literacy. The editors of *Rethinking Our Classrooms* (Bigelow, Christensen, Karp, Miner & Peterson, 1994) explain, "If we ask the children to critique the world but then fail to encourage them to act, our classrooms can degenerate into factories of cynicism. While it's not a teacher's role to direct students to particular organizations, it is a teacher's role to suggest that ideas need to be acted upon and to offer students opportunities to do just that" (p. 5).

During the 1996–1997 school year, Vasquez taught a half-day "junior kindergarten" in suburban Toronto, Canada, with 16 students between the ages of 3 and 5. For 10 months the students and teacher worked together to develop a critical literacy curriculum based on everyday texts and issues from their school and community. They created an *audit trail*, a bulletin board with artifacts, and commentary that visually documented their learning and the way incidents and themes flowed from one issue to another. Even though junior kindergarten is voluntary, the school board had a required curriculum from which Vasquez departed, yet she was careful to assure that the curriculum she negotiated with her students exceeded the requirements of the mandated program.

Rather than just adding social issues to a predetermined curriculum, Vasquez worked with her students to build their own course of study as they went—a dynamic approach that allowed them the flexibility to flow with student interest and connect ideas as they arose naturally. Barbara Comber (2001a) asserts that centering teaching on the concerns of the students and engaging local realities are crucial aspects of critical literacy. Some critics suggest that promoting a social justice agenda necessarily contradicts a student-centered curriculum. While this can be a bit of a balancing act, since negotiating curriculum with students requires listening as well as guiding, that does not mean that the two are contradictory. Carole Edelsky (1999) explains, "What makes a critical direction for a topic seem like an imposition of the teacher's agenda but a noncritical direction seem like neutral guidance is that the former disrupts prevailing ideologies" (p. 4).

Kathy Hall supports the idea of critical literacy playing a role in early childhood education, yet fears that if it dominates instruction it could "take the joy out of learning and living" and lead to cynicism (1998, p. 191). However, taking the pleasure out of learning is a problem that is more likely to occur when education fails to engage with students' interests, does not connect with their lived experiences, and provides them little opportunity to act on their learning. Vasquez's transformative pedagogy empowers children to actively engage with meaningful problems for the purpose of improving the situation. She writes, "The conversations that we had and the actions we took, although often serious, were very pleasurable. We enjoyed our work because the topics that we dealt with were socially significant to us" (1998, pp. 30–31).

This freedom to allow the curriculum to evolve in negotiation with the students is a luxury that Anderson and many teachers in the U.S. do not have without risking their employment. Especially now in the U.S., as NCLB promotes stringent accountability and high-stakes standardized testing, many teachers are mandated to teach from commercially produced scripted curriculum with predetermined pacing plans that aspire to have all children on the same page, on the same day, throughout a district. While integrating social issues into a core curriculum may be the only option many teachers have to bring progressive ideas to their students, Vasquez's work demonstrates an ideal situation. According to John Dewey (1938/1963), a defining characteristic that distinguishes progressive education based on experience from traditional banking education is that children's experiences are problematized and become the basis for learning. Dewey writes, "The new facts and new ideas thus obtained become the ground for further experiences in which new problems are presented. The process is a continuous spiral" (p. 79).

It is because of the current state of affairs of public education that the work Vasquez has done with young children is so important to demonstrate alternative pedagogy and the value of critical literacy. Vasquez organized her class around a daily meeting chaired by a student who followed an agenda of interests and concerns that students list before the meeting begins. Read-aloud literature is also shared daily and often generates topics for class discussion. At the beginning of the year, a children's book that Vasquez read prompted student interest in the rainforest, which led to letter writing action and the production of a rainforest play that highlighted the need to save the animals by not cutting down trees. On another occasion, an advertisement brought from home sparked media literacy analysis of the construction of advertising, which led to an inquiry of gender stereotypes and inspired some students to create alternative Halloween costumes.

During the year, different literature experiences and personal incidents set off the students on many critical inquiries and actions. Their exclusion from the French Café (a school event that most of the other students were able to enjoy) provoked feelings of anger and injustice. To protest their exclusion, they observed and surveyed other students to learn who else was not allowed to attend the French Café. Then they discussed their findings and considered having all the excluded students write letters to complain. Vasquez explained to the students that if all the letters were going to say the same thing, then a quicker option is to create a petition. Their interest in using literacy to solve a problem demonstrates the motivational power of an audience beyond the teacher and the value of having a genuine purpose for literacy activities. The students circulated their petition and then included it with an audiotape of their discussion about the French Café for the event organizers. Through their investigation and action, these young children exposed the power structure of the school and repositioned themselves within the hierarchy by using their collective voice. Vasquez writes, "My role was not to tell the children what to think or how to act, but based on their inquiries, to offer alternative ways of taking action and a way of naming their world within the stance they chose to take" (2004, p. 101).

Vasquez's stated goals of fairness and equality, along with the encouragement to problematize issues, built a strong sense of social justice in her students. When the class discovered after the annual school barbecue that one of their peers was not able to enjoy the food because only meat was available and he was a vegetarian, they moved into action. They began with a textual analysis of the flyer inviting people to the barbecue. The 3- and 4-year-old students challenged the use of the word "our" in the beginning of the text, "Join us for our Annual School Barbecue." Since the choice of hamburgers and hotdogs excluded vegetarians, the students insisted that the organizers were not being fair. This incident became a powerful opportunity for the students to apply the discursive analytic strategies that Vasquez had shown them before. She explains that previously they "had done some analysis of the words used in magazine ads and how pronouns work to position readers in particular ways" (2004, p. 104). In the letter to the chair of the school barbecue committee, the student chosen to write it decided to begin the letter using "we" instead of just mentioning the one vegetarian. When Vasquez questioned her about this choice, the young girl reminded her of the petition and explained to Vasquez about the strength in numbers. This understanding and application of pronouns goes well beyond most state standards for language arts skills in the upper grades.

The interests in the marginalization of vegetarians led the students to discover the complete absence of books about vegetarians in their school library. This, and curiosity about how other schools treat vegetarians, led Vasquez's students to send out many letters promoting vegetarian rights. She states that the letter-writing campaign "demonstrates what happens when young children begin to unpack the relationship between language and power by engaging in some form of discourse analysis" (2004, p. 111).

Teaching critical literacy involves vertical movement that encourages students to think more critically and analyze deeper the relationships between knowledge and power. Critical media literacy moves in this direction while also expanding horizontally to engage with many different forms of media and technology. The previous lessons about the French Café and the marginalization of vegetarians are excellent examples of critical literacy's vertical movement but barely expand the analysis horizontally to analyze and use different media and technology. In the next two examples, Vasquez engages her students with more of a critical media literacy perspective.

The first lesson began when one of her students spoke to the class about a news report she saw on television the night before. She told the other children about how pollution being dumped into a river was endangering the beluga whales that lived there. Based on this new knowledge, Vasquez decide, to revisit the picture book and song *Baby Beluga* by Raffi (1992), "to see whether they would read the book differently given what they had just learned" (2004, p. 113). The students compared the two texts and charted the different words used to describe the whales in the news report and the words used in the song. Vasquez explains, "In essence, what I was trying to do here was to get at the dominant themes and discourses of each text" (p. 115). This comparison triggered a student to ask "which one is real?" demonstrating how difficult it is for some children to distinguish between fantasy and reality. Vasquez used this problem to discuss different perspectives and how the construction of a text shapes the way we think. The students decided to rewrite Raffi's song to present more perspectives about belugas. During the process of rewriting the song, Vasquez led the students to explore issues of voice (who was speaking?), audience (who were they speaking to?), and construction (how were they using words to position the audience?). They experimented by swapping pronouns and changing all the verses of the song to read "you" instead of "I" or "we." This activity concretely demonstrated how easily they could change the voice of the author and the positioning of the audience by simply switching pronouns.

The students continued to research the plight of the beluga whales and performed their song to other students as a way of creating awareness for the dangers of pollution. They also raised money from their class store to donate to the World Wildlife Fund of Canada that was doing research to help the beluga. This critical media literacy activity began from student interest and involved analyzing different media representations as well as creating an alternative song. Vasquez explains that the power of this learning went well beyond just learning about whales, "[d]econstructing the book text and the everyday media text provided a space to explore the social construction of truth and reality" (p. 121).

By the time spring arrived, all of the 3-year-old students had turned 4 and many of the 4-year-olds were 5. They were also becoming better versed at critically interrogating texts as was apparent during a discussion about Mc-Donald's Happy Meal toys. A small group of students began discussing the way McDonald's has different toys for boys and girls. The students shared how the people working at McDonald's expected boys to prefer cars and girls to prefer dolls, but that they didn't always agree with that. This discussion about McDonald's gender bias and the students' ability to transgress it began a bigger critique of consumerism. The children discussed how McDonald's continually changes toys in order to lure kids to buy the Happy Meal in order to collect the new toy. One boy spoke with his father about this and later told the class that McDonald's claims that the toy is free but actually charges for it in the price of the Happy Meal. Through their discussions, the students were recognizing ways McDonald's targets them as consumers. They also questioned the fairness of McDonald's marketing strategies for children who do not have access to Happy Meal collectables.

Vasquez encouraged the students to explore deeper the construction of a consumer identity and worked with them to deconstruct the Happy Meal as a text. She drew a web with the golden arches in the center and then wrote the students' first responses in a circle around it to the question: "what makes up a Happy Meal?" After listing their initial comments (hamburger, French fries, bag, toy, and drink), she pushed them to think about all the things that are part of those items. The second concentric circle grew larger and more profound as the students mentioned advertising, designers, packaging, materials, and so on. This activity brilliantly addresses the essential media literacy concept that all media messages are constructed. Vasquez continued with a third concentric circle to expand further all the items related to those mentioned in the second circle. With each circle, the students were peeling away the unseen layers to reveal the complexity and subtexts of something as seemingly simple as a Happy Meal. Vasquez asserts that through critically questioning issues of gender and consumerism, her students were "disrupting taken-for-granted normality to consider how things could be different" (p. 131). This use of the students' culture and questions to deconstruct a media text, like the Happy Meal, is an excellent example of how critical media literacy can be taught through developmentally appropriate practices to young children. Experts in early childhood literacy assert that children learn literacy best, not by working in isolation, but through actively constructing meaning in an interactive and purposeful process (Neuman & Roskos, 2005a, 2005b).

Conclusion

Barbara Nicoll (1996) states, "From a developmental perspective, the process of growing toward being a critical thinker occurs very early in life. A necessary characteristic of critical thinkers is autonomy. As infants move into the autonomous stage of toddler hood the seeds of critical thinking have the potential to grow." Barbara Comber (2001b) asserts that when young children can learn to not only admire an author's crafting, but also disrupt it and see different possible representations, it can help children, who might not even be code-breakers, to start seeing texts as constructions and engage texts with deeper questions about the form as well as the content.

Unfortunately, many educators do not attempt to teach young children critical thinking skills and even fewer teach critical media literacy. The vast majority of U.S. educators have no idea what media literacy is and would not know how to begin to teach it. For the few who do know about critical media literacy, many do not teach it to young children because of the assumption that it is inappropriate, as was expressed in comments by Ms. Ramirez and Mr. Harvey in the previous chapter. Yet, the pedagogy used by Anderson and Vasquez are far more developmentally appropriate than many currently mandated phonics-based curricula. Some teachers might resist exposing young children to media out of fear that it is too dangerous and young children are too vulnerable, while other teachers might avoid critical pedagogy believing that teaching is a neutral activity and literacy just a technical competence. The primary goal of this chapter is to dispel those misconceptions and demonstrate through the outstanding work of two practicing teachers just how successful young children can be with multimedia literacy, computer literacy, critical literacy, and especially when it all comes together as critical media literacy. In an article presented on critical thinking in K–3 education, Nicoll concludes:

> Children need to develop an ability to recognize differing points of view and a willingness to explore alternatives. They need to be organized in their problem solving and

have good communication skills. The teacher's role is to create an atmosphere which encourages these attitudes. The teacher models open-mindedness, encourages differences of opinion, and asks for reasons for conclusions. Primary children will then be able to develop critical thinking skills and more importantly, critical thinking dispositions. (1996, p. 9)

Some of the real challenges for critical media literacy are to encourage educators to see media and popular culture as productive tools and texts for critical inquiry into issues of social justice as well as the opportunity to bridge the gap between "the real world" and the classroom. Key findings from research conducted in England with parents and early years practitioners suggest that both parents and early childhood educators feel that media education should be taught to young children. These researchers also found that "[t]he introduction of popular culture, media and/or new technologies into the communications, language and literacy curriculum has a positive effect on the motivation and engagement of children in learning" (Marsh et al., 2005, p. 6).

However, as we have seen, this type of pedagogical change is not easy with the current neoliberal policies that mandate accountability through high-stakes standardized testing and back-to-basics through skill and drill banking education. The challenge is significant but can be overcome when the obstacles are correctly identified. The real obstacles impeding critical media literacy are not children's deficiencies or media's danger; instead, they are the lack of backing and funding for the training and resources necessary to support teachers' exploration and implementation of critical media literacy pedagogy. The obstacles also include the lack of understanding and commitment to social justice and the development of empathy, empowerment, curiosity, and autonomy.

Mandates from above are needed to create space in the overcrowded curriculum for these ideas, and support at the school site is necessary to train and assist teachers in their efforts to integrate and transform their teaching practices to become more critical and inclusive. As Vasquez demonstrated from her teaching that flowed from student interests, critical media literacy needs official endorsement, but it cannot become a scripted cookbook of lessons. Vasquez writes:

there is no one-size-fits-all critical literacy . . . we need to construct different critical literacies depending on what work needs to be done in certain settings, contexts, or communities, and . . . it needs to be negotiated using the cultural and linguistic resources to which children have had access. (2003, p. 56)

Along with this mandate must come funding to pay for the training and for the purchasing of tools for students to create in multiple formats so that their voices and ideas can be heard and seen beyond the classroom. Anderson offered many examples of the production possibilities that 5 and 6 year olds are capable of creating. If we expand literacy beyond print to include popular culture, media, and technology and immerse that broader understanding of communication into a critical literacy framework, we have the potential to create transformative education for children from preschool on up. It is not enough to begin teaching critical media literacy to teenagers; we must start as early as possible, even if we are just planting seeds. Building awareness of how media operate, how we interact with ICTs, how ideas and culture are socially constructed, and how power is linked to all these processes is essential if we hope to create a world of media literate citizens who can participate in the struggle to recover democracy and transform society into a more equal and just place to live.

CHAPTER SIX

Thinking Critically in a Converging World

Forces of Change in the Information Age

This book has explored the theoretical underpinnings of critical media literacy, examined some of the obstacles for implementing progressive pedagogical changes, and provided examples of practical applications. A multiperspectival approach addressing issues of gender, race, class, and power has been used to explore the interconnections of cultural studies, critical pedagogy, and critical media literacy. The battle for representative democracy and social justice must be fought at every level, and people of all ages should be learning critical media literacy concepts through a transformative pedagogy to help them engage in this struggle. In the previous chapters, the question of *how* to best teach critical media literacy to elementary school students was examined. Although the question assumes that media literacy should be taught, that assumption has yet to occur to the majority of U.S. educators and policy makers. For that reason, this final chapter begins by discussing some of the major changes in media and society in the past few decades. These changes require a new pedagogy that can engage with the forces of globalization, new technologies, and different epistemologies.

In the 21st century, critical media literacy is an imperative for participatory democracy because new ICTs and a market-based media culture have fragmented, connected, converged, diversified, homogenized, flattened, broadened, and reshaped the world. These changes have been reframing the way people think and restructuring societies at local and global levels. A new epistemological framework for literacy education is now necessary because of the rapid growth of ICT, the expansion of free market global capitalism, and the escalating and vanishing linguistic and cultural diversity that is changing social environments at local as well as global levels.

Looking at the impact of globalization on identity, Manuel Castells (2004) asserts that people's lives are being shaped by the forces of the network society. He suggests that the interconnections between technology, economics, culture, and identity are challenging, conflicting, and impacting upon each other on a global scale. Castells writes:

> The information technology revolution, and the restructuring of capitalism, have induced a new form of society, the network society. It is characterized by the globalization of strategically decisive economic activities. By the networking form of organization. By the flexibility and instability of work, and the individualization of labor. By a culture of real virtuality constructed by a pervasive, interconnected, and diversified media system. And by the transformation of the material foundations of life, space and time, through the constitution of a space of flows and of timeless time, as expressions of dominant activities and controlling elites. (2004, p. 1)

Already in the 1960s, Marshall McLuhan argued that many of the characteristics of the premodern oral age will again rise up in importance as the instantaneous and continuous electronic age proves to be more similar to oral cultures of the ancient past than the last centuries of typographic literacy. He wrote these ideas before the existence of cellular phones, the Internet, and HDTV, yet today, as the World Wide Web and wireless communication become commonplace in most first world countries, as well as in many parts of the developing world, his words echo more true now than when he first wrote them a half century ago.

According to McLuhan (1997), before print literacy, humans were hunters and gatherers living in oral societies with tribal cultures that were unified, inclusive, auditory, organic, and had high levels of participation. With the invention of the phonetic alphabet, a new era began. Literacy caused the eye to replace the ear, and the cosmic culture became fragmented and separated by a new system of repeatability and uniformity. In the 15th century these changes exploded with the invention of Gutenberg's printing press. McLuhan calls this the "mechanical age" and attributes the arrival of individualism, rationalism, and nationalism to this new print literate culture of homogeneity and lineal organization.

The next great change for humanity, according to McLuhan, came with the discovery of electricity and the invention of the telegraph. The new electronic age has and continues to cause an implosion on society that is returning humans to their earlier oral roots. This latest age of automation and cybernation takes us back to a more participative, integral, decentralized, and inclusive way of living. McLuhan asserts that electricity, with its speed and constancy, is the medium that created simultaneity; it is an extension of our central nervous system, "instantly interrelating every human experience" (p. 358). He suggests that all media are extensions of ourselves; the print is an extension of the eye as the wheel is an extension of the foot.

Now more than ever, we are seeing the transformation of societies into what McLuhan coined the "global village," and the electronic age that he spoke of is in full force, reshaping societies and identities across the globe. For today's literate society to keep pace with the age of information, education must let go of curriculum that is separated by subjects and change over "to an interrelation in knowledge," asserts McLuhan (p. 35). He asks, "Would it not seem natural and necessary that the young be provided with at least as much training of perception in this graphic and photographic world as they get in the typographic? In fact, they need more training in graphics, because the art of casting and arranging actors in ads is both complex and forcefully insidious" (p. 230).

Adding economic and technological determinist perspectives to McLuhan's technological determinism, Thomas Friedman (2005) argues that at the turn of this millennium, humans entered the third major shift in globalizing change. He writes that the first great era of globalization began in 1492 when Columbus opened trade between the New World and the Old. During what Friedman calls Globalization 1.0, imperialism and religion drove global integration through brute force as colonizing countries deployed the labor power of exploited peoples until about 1800. The second era, Globalization 2.0, ran from about 1800 to 2000 and involved multinational companies expanding their markets and labor forces as industrialization reshaped the world. This second era benefited first from the decrease in transportation costs and later from the decrease in telecommunication costs and was marked by the inventions of new hardware. Yet, in the 21st century, Friedman claims that Globalization 3.0 is driven by innovative software and a global fiber optic network and asserts that the unique character of this era is "the newfound power for *individuals* to collaborate and compete globally" (p. 10).

His claim that the world is now less hierarchical with a more level playing field than ever before is overly ideological and optimistic; Friedman is too uncritical of inequalities and injustices of neoliberal globalization (Klein, 2007). However, his assertion that "the world has been flattened by the convergence of ten major political events, innovations, and companies" (p. 48) is highly provocative and highlights many recent changes in society that are having a global impact. His utopian conclusion that the world is now flat and there is more equal opportunity is unfounded since one third of the world's population still lives without electricity. Yet, Friedman's discussion of the major forces that have changed the world in just the last couple of decades makes it clear that the 21st century is a different world and will continue to change because of influences of new ICTs and global economic systems. The examples he describes of transformations in technology, society, and economy provide strong reasons for the need to change education and especially literacy practices. The type of changes that would best accommodate a globalized world perpetually transformed by technology include multiple literacies, of which critical media literacy is essential.

The diversity of ideas and people is increasing in countries, cities, and classrooms as escalating amounts of information become available and larger numbers of people travel and immigrate across the globe. At the same time, there is a reduction of diversity as cultural colonialization and commercial homogenization spread throughout the global markets with the ease of new ICTs. One example of the loss of diversity can be seen in UNESCO's warning that, "Over 50% of the world's 6000 languages are endangered" with one disappearing almost every other week.[1] Joseph Lo Bianco (2000) states that "During this and the next decade there will be the greatest collapse of language diversity in all history" (p. 94). He attributes these changes to an emerging global system being generated by three principal forces: "The first is the almost universal phenomenon of market deregulation; the second is the advanced integration of international financial markets; and the third is the critical facilitating force of instantaneous communications" (p. 93).

One of the common themes running through many analyses of the changes in the relationship between media and society is a high degree of *convergence* that is occurring in numerous ways (Considine, 2003; Gutiérrez, 2003; Jenkins, 2006; Luke, 2007). Henry Jenkins (2006) insists that we are now living in a *convergence culture*, in which our sociocultural practices are changing because of the influences of technology and economics, and convergence of old and new media. He explains, "Media convergence is more than simply a technological shift. Convergence alters the relationship between existing technologies, industries, markets, genres, and audiences" (p. 15). Jenkins highlights two major and often contradictory trends, one in which large media corporations threaten democracy by their concentration of ownership, giving fewer people a greater ability to push and amplify their limited content out to the masses while new media technologies have made it easier on a grassroots level for more people to pull, create, and distribute much more diverse media content, thereby offering new opportunities for democracy. This dynamic push and pull of media is a key aspect of convergence and something Jenkins states, "represents a paradigm shift—a move from medium-specific content toward content that flows across multiple media channels, toward the increased interdependence of communications systems, toward multiple ways of accessing media content, and toward ever more complex relations between top-down corporate media and bottom-up participatory culture" (p. 243).

These changes in technology and society are shaping the way people think and relate to media. Jenkins asserts that the larger problem for educators today is not the old notion of a digital divide that separates people based on limited access to the tools of communication, since more people have access today than ever before, but the larger problem today is a *participation gap*, "the unequal access to the opportunities, experiences, skills, and knowledge that will prepare youth for full participation in the world of tomorrow" (Jenkins, Purushotma, Clinton, Weigel & Robison, 2007, p. 3). Jenkins writes, "We need to rethink the goals of media education so that young people can come to think of themselves as cultural producers and participants and not simply as consumers, critical or otherwise" (2006, p. 259).

Framing the changes in technological and social terms, Carmen Luke (2007) argues for an expanded form of media literacy because of three increasingly growing levels of media convergence. One level of convergence is the functional ability of hardware devices to perform multiple tasks, such as a cell phone that can take and send pictures (still and moving images), play music, send and receive text messages, upload and download content online, play games, and can still be used for chatting. A second level of media convergence entails provider convergence that has been greatly enhanced by deregulations of media ownership and the numerous mergers and acquisitions of multinational media corporations. The horizontal and vertical integration of media companies allows fewer corporations the ability to control more different types of services and content (Bagdikian, 2004; McChesney, 2004). The ability of ICTs to perform more functions and the integration of media providers are also contributing to *transmedia intertextuality* (Kinder, 1991).

According to Luke, the third level of media convergence is a consequence of the two previously mentioned that have had the effect of creating "a much tighter synergy between previously disparate industries, between knowledge

and information, consumerism, popular culture, entertainment, communication, and education" (2007, p. 52). As politics, news, and entertainment con-
verge into new forms of media, an entire spectator culture is evolving. Douglas
Kellner writes that "spectacle itself is becoming one of the organizing principles of the economy, polity, society, and everyday life" (2006b). He asserts
that in order to grab larger audiences and increase profit and power, the culture
industries aggressively create and promote a synthesized spectacle-centered
media culture.

Buckingham echoes Luke's analysis of the multiple levels of convergence
when he writes, "The proliferation of media technologies, the commercialization and globalization of media markets, the fragmentation of mass audiences
and the rise of 'interactivity' are all fundamentally transforming young people's
everyday experiences with media" (2003, p. 15). Luke suggests that these con-
vergences require different types of literacies and thought processes:

> Thinking laterally across associations, developing a meta-awareness of the links or
> paths taken and those passed over, backtracking along paths, reading and viewing
> mix-and-match old and new blended media genres and forms—these are the very
> rhizomatic conceptual and cognitive maps required to read through and think through
> localized branchings of larger global knowledge units (disciplinary or otherwise).
> Thinking across associations, accessing, and integrating knowledge laterally are the
> very cognitive, socially situated repertoires we use to negotiate everyday life and are
> core requirements for hypertext navigation. (2006, p. 272)

James Paul Gee (2000) suggests that technological innovations and hyper-
competitive global "fast capitalism" are creating a new type of individual whom
he calls the "portfolio person" (p. 43). Gee explains that the idea of "expertise"
has moved "away from 'disciplinary' or academic expertise to a broader notion
more compatible with the new capitalist world view" (p. 48). He writes that
this business orientation, much like Friedman's flat world perspective, emphasizes

> efficient problem solving, productivity, innovation, adaptation, and non-authoritarian
> distributed systems . . . In the new capitalism, it is not really important what individu-
> als know on their own, but rather what that they can do with others collaboratively to
> effectively add 'value' to the enterprise. (Gee, 2000, p. 49)

A problem with this education of the portfolio person is that it is based on
a cognitive notion of knowledge workers who have the facility of "higher order
thinking" but lack the ability to think critically about issues of social justice.
Gee labels this as the ability to think *critiquely*, "to understand and critique systems of power and injustice" (p. 62). The inability to understand or empathize

with marginalized, poor, and oppressed people is a major problem of this fast capitalism epistemology.

Another problem with the model that creates the portfolio person is that it advantages most the children from dominant positions in society (i.e., white, male, middle or upper class), who have easier access to this expertise and "school language" based on their lifeworld experiences and privileges. It is much easier to bridge the home culture to the public school domain for students who have been exposed to white middle-class values such as reading children's literature from an early age or visiting museums and art galleries. The common deficit thinking approach that many educators internalize undervalues the cultural assets that minority and poor students bring to school and often frame those resources as problems to be overcome (Valencia & Solorzano, 2004). Gee writes,

> We rarely build on their experiences and on their very real distinctive lifeworld knowledge. In fact, they are often asked, in the process of being exposed to specialist domains, to deny the value of their lifeworlds and their communities in reference to those of more advantaged children. (2000, p. 66)

To counteract the problems of inequality and lack of social critique, Gee promotes a Bill of Rights for all students that includes four pedagogical principles: situated practices, overt instruction, critical framing, and transformative practice. He writes, "These principles seek to produce people who can function in the new capitalism, but in a much more meta-aware and political fashion than forms of new-capitalist-complicit schooling" (p. 67). The situated practice can help value the different cultural capital (Bourdieu, 1986) students bring into the classroom as child-centered experiential practices allow students to discover connections between their lifeworlds and school. A major aspect of these principles is a metacognitive awareness about the interconnections of thinking, knowledge, and power relations. The need for some overt instruction and critical framing assures that students will engage with texts critiquely to understand the interconnections and systems of power.

The fourth principle of transformed practice suggests that education must involve acting on learning and empower students to use and transform knowledge. When Gee's fourth principle of transformative practice is built on critical framing, then Jenkins's goal of bridging the participation gap can become a reconstruction of education promoting critical media literacy. In a report funded by the MacArthur Foundation, Jenkins and others assert the need for teaching

> new media literacies: a set of cultural competencies and social skills that young people need in the new media landscape. Participatory culture shifts the focus of literacy from one of individual expression to community involvement. The new literacies almost all involve social skills developed through collaboration and networking. These skills build on the foundation of traditional literacy, research skills, technical skills, and critical analysis skills taught in the classroom. (Jenkins et al., 2007, p. 4)

These pedagogical principles that Gee proposes provide excellent suggestions for *how* critical media literacy should be taught and are in line with many of John Dewey's and Paulo Freire's philosophies. In Chapter Two, critical media literacy was described as consisting of many components of different types of media education and involves *conceptual understandings* (Buckingham, 2003) based largely on theoretical ideas from cultural studies (Durham & Kellner, 2002). These concepts are meant to empower students with the tools to critically analyze messages and use popular culture, new technologies, and media to create their own representations. When applied to challenging social injustice and based on critical cultural studies, critical media literacy can be a powerful tool for radical democracy and social change. Kellner (1995) writes, "A critical cultural studies conceptualizes society as a terrain of domination and resistance and engages in a critique of domination and of the ways that media culture engages in reproducing relationships of domination and oppression" (p. 4). Len Masterman (1996) suggests that media education "should aspire to be an effective education in human rights" because the politics of representation require communication and interpretive rights that are linked to civil, political, economic, and social rights (p. 74). He states, "in contemporary societies widespread media literacy is a pre-requisite for the defence, preservation and extension of human rights" (p. 77).

Tackling social justice issues of power inequality is extremely important for media educators since media today are creating and disseminating some of the most ubiquitous and oppressive representations of white supremacy, patriarchy, homophobia, and classism. This is all the more pernicious in a society like ours, where these ideas become naturalized as part of the hegemonic ideology echoed and promoted in all the major social institutions (family, church, state, schools, and media). Robyn Quin and Barrie McMahon (2003) write:

> Integral to questions of identity are issues of power. The ways in which relations of power and subordination are signified with media representations of sexuality, gender, race, and disability need to be set alongside questions of individual and cultural identity. Power is implicated too in questions about who or what groups have the power to define specific issues of identity whether this be the power of the news editor to include or exclude a story or the power of the film director to selectively represent heroes as white males. (p. 124)

One of the great successes of the positivist neoconservative discourse is that the focus on back-to-basics has shifted the goals of education away from progressive social justice concerns toward conservative banking concepts of memorization, standardization, and assessment. The emphasis on accountability based on standardized test scores has disempowered teachers and hindered their creativity by putting them into the role of task managers and test trainers rather than professional pedagogues exciting youth with ideas and curiosity. To move from this conservative agenda, or even a liberal framework, to radical problem-posing social justice pedagogy is unpopular in today's political climate and is more difficult to implement than an apolitical version of media literacy. Robert Ferguson writes, "For the opposite of political consciousness is not political unconsciousness but apolitical consciousness. I would further suggest that the apolitically conscious usually side with the forces of domination in a given social formation" (1998, p. 23).

Bringing a sociological perspective that challenges these injustices into elementary school classrooms can be a challenge. It is often difficult to convince K–12 teachers to use media literacy to engage with problems of racism, sexism, homophobia, and classism. Some believe that these issues are not developmentally appropriate for young children, but the work discussed in the previous chapter demonstrated that it is in fact possible and appropriate. Many teachers are overworked and undersupported. As their jobs increasingly depend on high-stakes tests, they worry more about assessment and job security than idealistic notions of changing the world. The current atmosphere of fear, which SMARTArt teachers described in their interviews, influences how and what they teach along with the amount of experimentation they are willing to risk. This climate is not conducive to supporting teachers who want to transform their curriculum to pose problems of racism, sexism, classism, or homophobia. Often, these types of politicizing activities are frowned upon and seen as personal agendas that divert children from learning the skills they need to get jobs in the "real world." In 2003, a *Los Angeles Times Magazine* cover story attacked a charter middle school with a social justice agenda, suggesting that it was struggling "with the fine line between teaching social justice and the force-feeding of political indoctrination" (Colvin, 2003, p. 13). The speed and ease of corporate media to label progressive education as indoctrination while treating conservative banking pedagogy as neutral makes it all the more difficult for educators to raise issues of social justice with their students.

Even though the media's spin on the term *indoctrination* is often used politically unevenly and naïvely undervalues human agency, it does raise concerns about the necessity for social justice to be taught through democratic problem-posing pedagogy. Using a banking methodology to impart social justice values is deeply flawed because it teaches students to do the same noncritical regurgitation of decontextualized information but with different content. A democratic pedagogy should be child centered and allowed to flow from students' interests, experiences, and questions. A misplaced understanding of democratic pedagogy leads some educators to believe that there should be no direct instruction and that only topics originating from students are legitimate for study. These educators sometimes use this as an excuse not to bring issues of racism, sexism, classism, or homophobia into a classroom where students have not already expressed an interest. The logic of this argument would lead to an education that would never advance beyond the small world that students already occupy. Gee (2000) points out that situated practices also require overt instruction to scaffold and guide academic objectives. Along with this guidance, Gee asserts the need for teachers to provide students with critical framing and the possibility to create and transform knowledge. This is a difficult balancing act in which democratic pedagogy encourages teachers to lessen their overt instruction and diminish their power over students, yet this does not mean abdicating the role of leader and guide. Good democratic pedagogues work with students to build bridges and help them find the connections between their lifeworlds and the academic goals that must include social justice. Within democratic child-centered pedagogy, teachers should pose problems to their students in order for them to wrestle with the issues and come to conclusions that they believe are socially just. Howard Zinn (1990) suggests that educators should pose the questions to guide the exploration but not the final conclusions. Education should be a process of exploration and discovery, rather than an accumulation of isolated skills and facts.

Standpoint theory is a research methodology that can be useful as pedagogy for encouraging students to begin questioning from positions of subordination with the intention of illuminating the power structure of the information as well as alternative perspectives. This approach is easiest with students who themselves inhabit marginalized positions since it can emerge from their experiences and connect to their lifeworlds. Such an approach is more difficult to use with students accustomed to the privileges that come with inhabiting dominant positions. This raises a difficult question: How do you bring someone from a dominant perspective to consider and appreciate counterhegemonic ideas? In this culture, the challenge is greatest with white, straight, male, middle-class teachers and students who enjoy the privileges and benefits from pertaining to the dominant race, class, gender, and sexual preference. Often, people in these dominant positions do not recognize the oppression that others face and are resistant to empathizing with the plight of the oppressed. At the same time, people in marginalized positions tend to have more ability to see the negative effects and structure of oppression as well as having more incentive to want to change the injustice. Although everyone will benefit from a society that is more socially just, this is something that is more difficult to convince people about if they do not directly feel the negative effects of oppression and exploitation. It is the indirect or long-range effects, such as increasing violence because of escalating unemployment or global warming because of unlimited consumption and destruction of natural resources, that are very real but more complicated to prove.

One possible solution is to follow SMARTArt teacher Mr. Baker's lead in building empathy with his students through providing primary sources from people in subordinate positions who have experienced oppression and discrimination. The diaries his students read about the Japanese Americans imprisoned at the Manzanar Internment Camp during World War II provided firsthand experiences with visceral examples of injustice that his students could relate to on personal levels. The teacher demonstrated excellent critical framing by helping his students connect this learning with current situations. This fits with standpoint theory's methodology of beginning inquiry from a subordinate position. It also joins well with Ferguson's goal of critical solidarity (2001) that aims to expose the interconnections of all ideas and systems. Luke (2006) writes, "In digitized knowledge and networked environments, an understanding of the relations among ideas is as [important] if not more important than mastery of the bare facts. The conceptual shift here is one from *collection* to *connection*" (p. 272). This valuing of the connections and interdependence of ideas and people was brought onto an international stage when former U.S. president Bill Clinton spoke to the British Labour Party conference and proclaimed the need to embrace the African concept of *ubuntu*. Originating from the Bantu languages that are spoken in Southern Africa, ubuntu translates as "I am because you are" (Coughlan, 2006).

This movement requires more than just changing curricula; it requires changing pedagogy; educators must learn to teach differently. Creating transparency in the classroom about how power is enacted between the teacher and students is an important step. This type of discussion may be easier to do with older children but should be considered by all teachers as one way to help them lessen their role as expert and encourage students to join into the educational process as active participants. Students should be taught about the powers they have as young citizens and encouraged to use their agency in life and in the classroom to speak up about issues that concern them and question the problems that disturb them. This type of transparency depends on self-reflection by the teacher and the students. A metacognitve self-actualizing approach that helps students think about thinking and reflect on their own beliefs can benefit deeper inquiry for critical thinking (hooks, 1994).

While confronting issues of social injustice can make teaching uncomfortable and more difficult, it is this type of discomfort that Ferguson (1998) asserts we most need in education, a sense of *productive unease*. We need to engage students in dilemmas and contradictions so they can explore and wrestle with issues that matter to them, thereby making learning relevant and meaningful. Simply exposing students to problems is not enough, as Gee reminds us of the need for overt instruction and critical framing to accompany situated practice. Much can be gained by combining Ferguson's notion of productive unease with Neil Mercer's (2007) understanding of the sociocultural importance of conversation and questioning in order to develop collective thinking. Mercer suggests that students need to be taught how to use "exploratory" ways of communicating and thinking collaboratively. He writes, "Exploratory talk, with its explicit reasons, criticisms and evaluations, is a model of dialogue in which participants are not primarily concerned with protecting their separate identities and interests, but instead with ways of jointly and rationally making sense" (Mercer, 2007, p. 173). Teaching students metacognitive skills about communication and thinking can help them independently and collaboratively address problems being posed to them. In order for the unease to become productive and skepticism not to sink into cynicism, students need to build their metacognitive awareness and sense of agency as they take action to create solutions for the problems they encounter.

Critical media literacy that is based on critical pedagogy should lead students to doubt, investigate, reflect, and create in critical solidarity with others who are oppressed by the effects of hegemony and injustice. The need to disrupt the author's power and challenge all texts is essential for laying the foundation of critical thinking that understands all messages are co-constructed and can be re-constructed differently. Empowering students to think critically and sociologically depends on more than merely introducing concepts of racism and sexism; it depends on the practice of doubting, questioning, challenging, and wondering about other ways of being and thinking. The concept of productive unease holds much potential for allowing constructivist pedagogy to be child centered and still problem posing. By expanding students' interests and concerns with a sense of productive unease, teachers can guide students to engage with personal issues and challenge them to discover the connections their concerns have in critical solidarity with others in subordinated positions.

From the case study of Project SMARTArt teachers, the most recurring comment that all the teachers expressed had to do with their belief in the importance of media literacy education. This is almost ironic in light of the other most common remark about how little media literacy they are actually teaching now. Their strong understanding of the theoretical base and current need for media education clashes with the current realities they face daily that require them to use scripted curriculum and follow a mandated schedule. The positivist influence of accountability and standardization is clearly impeding most of these teachers from experimenting, taking risks, using their own creativity, and bringing new ideas into the classroom. This is disheartening.

However, the teachers also mentioned the shining moments when media literacy made a difference for their students and the occasions when it still sneaks into their curriculum from time to time. The teachers also provided many excellent suggestions for what is needed for media literacy to systematically become integrated into elementary school education. Most of their ideas, like thematic teaching and project-based learning, follow the theoretical advice discussed throughout this book. They also mentioned the wonderful opportunity that media education can provide special education students. The teachers discussed the importance of media literacy for motivating student interest, promoting metacognition, encouraging students to think outside the box, and consider different perspectives necessary to build empathy, as well as teaching many of the goals necessary for learning critical autonomy and critical solidarity.

Conclusion

Throughout the U.S., small pockets of educators are teaching lessons in media literacy to fortunate students; however, in order to do this, they often have to struggle against many obstacles rather than being supported and encouraged. The role of good administrators and policy makers should be to remove the obstacles and create the support that will best assist progressive educators who want to teach for radical democracy as well as encourage those educators who want to make a difference but just do not know how. The SMARTArt teachers demonstrated and expressed the advice that educators must be respected and trusted to use their independent judgment, creativity, and passion to ignite the imaginations of their students and make learning transformative and pleasurable for all involved.

Cultural studies and critical pedagogy offer the theoretical background to inform practice that can transform education and society. To move forward with critical media literacy, we need to lobby for better funding for education, especially where it is needed most in the inner cities. We need to challenge the false wisdom of high-stakes testing and deficit thinking, as well as to train teachers in critical pedagogy and empower them to use their creativity more than the scripted curricula. In addition, we need conferences, teacher education, and continuing professional development that teach cultural studies, critical pedagogy, and practical applications for how to engage students in the classroom with critical media literacy concepts.

Currently, media literacy policy in the U.S. is in its formative years and has advanced little during the Bush–Cheney era. Needed policy challenges include overcoming the conservative and neoliberal hegemony and coming up with democratic and progressive alternatives. Federal and state grants for experimental projects in media literacy can be extremely beneficial and should be pursued by educators. National and state conferences that specifically address the teaching of critical media literacy can provide excellent places for progressive educators and policy makers to unite and work together, sharing and building a movement. Parent groups should provide their members with resources and discussions to address the concerns they have about media and how they can teach critical media literacy in the home. Parent organizations should also use their collective power to influence school curriculum and lobby Congress in support of progressive education.

Media education programs should be instituted from preschool and throughout K–12. Media literacy must be linked with production as a regular practice. Standards for media literacy programs should include criticizing the ways that media reproduce racism, sexism, homophobia, and other prejudices and encouraging students to find their own voices in criticizing media culture and producing alternative media. Media education should be linked with education for democracy where students are encouraged to become informed and media-literate participants in their societies. Media literacy should thus be linked with information literacy, technological literacy, the arts, and the social sciences. Critical media literacy should be a common thread that runs through all curricular areas since it deals with communication and society.

The basis of media literacy is that all messages are constructed, and when education begins with this understanding of the social construction of knowledge, the literacy process can expand critical inquiry into multiple forms of information and communication, including television programs, Internet, advertising, popular culture, media, and books. Literacy is thus a necessary condition to equip people to participate in the local, national, and global economy; culture; and polity. As Dewey (1916/1997) argued, education is necessary to enable people to participate in democracy, for without an educated, informed, and literate citizenry, strong democracy is impossible. Moreover, there are crucial links between literacy, democracy, empowerment, and social participation in politics and everyday life. Hence, without developing adequate literacies, differences between "haves" and "have nots" cannot be overcome and individuals and groups will be left out of the emerging global economy and networked society.

In the global village, it is not enough to merely understand media; students need to be empowered to critically negotiate meanings, engage with the problems of misrepresentations and underrepresentations, and produce their own alternative media. Addressing issues of inequality and injustice in media representations can be a powerful starting place for problem-posing transformative education. Critical media literacy offers the tools and framework to help students become subjects in the process of deconstructing injustices, expressing their own voices, and struggling to create a better society.

Education must move from collection to connection (Luke, 2006) and from a psychological model of instruction to a sociological one (Luke & Freebody, 1997). We need a new exploratory language and framework for teachers and students to think metacognitively about literacy, social justice, media, and society. Analysis must be inseparable from action as students apply their ideas in praxis to transform injustice and improve society. Critical media literacy can offer a framework for moving education in that direction when it is based on cultural studies, critical pedagogy, feminist theory, and critical literacy. Working with young students holds the potential for planting the necessary seeds for a radical democracy built upon the type of critical autonomy and critical solidarity that will empower responsible and caring citizens to actively shape democracy.

MediaLit Kit™
Framework

Center for Media Literacy's MediaLit Kit™

	Core concepts	Key questions	Questions to guide young children
1	All media messages are "constructed"	Who created this message?	What is this? How is this put together?
2	Media messages are constructed using a creative language with its own rules	What techniques are used to attract my attention?	What do I see, hear, smell, touch, or taste? What do I like or dislike about this?
3	Different people experience the same media message differently	How might different people understand this message differently from me?	What do I think and feel about this? What might other people think and feel about this?
4	Media have embedded values and points of view	What lifestyles, values, and points of view are represented or omitted in this message?	What does this tell me about how other people live and believe? Is anything or anyone left out?
5	Media are organized to gain profit and/or power	Why was this message sent?	Is this trying to tell me something? Is this trying to sell me something?

Critical Media Literacy Chart

Critical media literacy needs to begin with an understanding and acceptance that all education is political, and it should be taught through a democratic pedagogy that respects civil rights and the principles of social justice

	Critical media literacy involves . . .	Conceptual understandings	Prompts
1	recognition of the *construction of media messages as a social process*, rather than accepting texts as neutral or transparent conveyors of information	*Social constructivism* All information is co-constructed by individuals and groups of people within social contexts	What contexts affect the message of the media text?
2	a semiotic *textual analysis* that explores languages, genres, codes, and conventions of all texts (digital, visual, audio, print based, etc.)	*Languages* Media use languages with specific codes and conventions	How is the media text put together?
3	an exploration of the roles audiences play in actively "negotiating meanings" and how audiences contribute to positioning themselves in the meaning-making process	*Audience* Individuals and groups understand media messages similarly and/or differently	What are different ways the media text could be understood?
4	an examination of the process of *representation*, to uncover and engage issues of bias, point of view, ideology, omission, aesthetics, power, and pleasure in the content of the text	*Representation* Media have embedded ideologies, discourses, and points of view that convey hierarchical power relations	What are different messages, either obvious or subtle, that can be read in the media text?

(Continued on following page.)

	Critical media literacy involves . . .	Conceptual understandings	Prompts
5	studying the *institutions and systems* that motivate and structure the mass media locally and globally, which for the most part are corporate businesses whose primary goal is maximizing profit	*Production/institutions* Most media are commercially motivated and organized within global capitalism or state control of broadcasting	Why was the media text created and why was it sent?
6	the foregrounding of *identity markers* of race, class, gender, sexuality, etc., as a way to question and challenge the role media texts play in perpetuating racist, classist, sexist, homophobic, and other socially unjust ideas, practices, and institutions, as well as the valorization of representations that present nonracist, nonsexist, nonhomophobic, and other positive representations of subordinate groups that are often represented in stereotyped or offensive ways	*Identity* Media shape and influence identity formation through repetition of hegemonic discourses. Media culture is a terrain of struggle between different groups played out in media culture and so media literacy shows how media plays out these struggles, often in entertainment	Who or what group is benefiting and who or what group is suffering from this media text?

SMARTArt Teacher Pseudonyms and Descriptions

SMARTArt teachers interviewed	Number of years with grant	Special ed or regular ed	Still teaching a class: Yes or no	Gender: Male or female	Grade level they taught during grant
Ms. Brown	3	SE	Y	F	3–5
Ms. Hernandez	3	R	Y	F	2
Ms. Martin	3	R	Y	F	3
Mr. Harvey	3	R	N (coordinator at different school)	M	3
Ms. Rogers	2	R	Y	F	2
Ms. Hendrix	2	SE	Y (resource teacher at different school)	F	2–4
Ms. Ramirez	2	R	N (literacy coach at different school)	F	2
Ms. Smith	1 (3rd year)	SE	Y	F	1–3
Ms. Jones	2	R	N (retired)	F	4
Mr. Baker	2	R	Y	M	3

(Continued on following page.)

SMARTArt teachers interviewed	Number of years with grant	Special ed or regular ed	Still teaching a class: Yes or no	Gender: Male or female	Grade level they taught during grant
Ms. Vargas	2	R	N (literacy coach)	F	2
Mr. Ruiz	1 (3rd year)	R	Y	M	4
Mr. Gomez	1 (2nd year)	R	Y	M	3
Mr. Shaw	2	SE	Y (different school)	M	K–2

Interview Guide

1. If a friend asked you what "media literacy" is, how would you define it?
2. What aspects of media literacy (key questions, core concepts, democratic pedagogy, etc.) do you find most useful and why?
3. Are you now using what you learned from the media literacy grant? If so, how?
4. Do you think your teaching practices have become more critical since this grant? If so, how?
5. Do you believe that your students are developing better questions that reflect more critical thinking? If so, why?
6. What benefit do you think production activities play in student learning media literacy?
7. What do you consider your most successful media literacy moments?
8. What major obstacles keep you from teaching more media literacy?
9. What do you think are the best ways to integrate critical media literacy into elementary school curriculum?
10. Do you have any suggestions for me related to media literacy or is there anything else you would like to add?
11. In terms of social justice issues, racism, classism, sexism, how do you address that, or do you address those types of things, with your students?

Notes

Chapter One

1. The U.S. Census Bureau reports that 98.2 percent of all US households had at least one television set in 2004 and 54.6 percent of all U.S. households had computers with Internet access in 2003. Retrieved October 6, 2008, from http://www.census.gov/prod/2006pubs/07statab/infocomm.pdf
2. These 25 lesson plans correspond with the 5 core concepts, 5 lessons per concept. These lesson plans are available in both English and Spanish. All the lessons are available online for free at the Center for Media Literacy's Web site. Retrieved August 17, 2008, from http://www.medialit.org/reading_room/article661.html
3. The case study can be accessed online. Retrieved August 17, 2008, from http://www.medialit.org/reading_room/article659.html

Chapter Two

1. The 10 educators who make up The New London Group are Courtney Cazden, Bill Cope, Norman Fairclough, Jim Gee, Mary Kalantzis, Gunther Kress, Allen Luke, Carmen Luke, Sarah Michaels, and Martin Nakata.
2. In 2007, the two national U.S. media literacy organizations boasted memberships of only

about 400 people each.

3. NAMLE formerly the Alliance for a Media Literate America (AMLA) posts this definition of media literacy on their Web site. Retrieved August 17, 2008 from http://www.amlainfo.org/media-literacy/definitions

4. I attended this class as a student during my first quarter at UCLA, and later I was the teaching associate for the class during the Fall 2005 quarter. Hammer's course Web site was retrieved August 17, 2008 from http://www.sscnet.ucla.edu/05F/womencm178-1/

5. Canada's Ontario Ministry of Education's Eight Key Concepts, British Film Institute's (BFI) Signpost Questions, The Center for Media Literacy's Five Core Concepts, and so on.

6. Ontario Ministry of Education. (1989). *Media literacy resource guide: Intermediate and senior divisions* (pp. 8–10). Toronto, Canada.

7. Hart, A. (Ed.). (1998). *Teaching the media: International perspectives* (p. 13). Mahwah, NJ: Lawrence Erlbaum. Hart attributes the source of the BFI Signpost Questions to Bazalgette, C. (Ed.). (1989). *Primary media education: A curriculum statement* (p. 8). London: British Film Institute.

8. The CML framework is referred to as the *MediaLit Kit*™ and was retrieved August 17, 2008 from http://www.medialit.org/pdf/mlk_orientationguide.pdf. These same concepts can also be found in Masterman's list of general areas for investigation in his theoretical framework (2001, pp. 20–21).

9. An example of an analysis activity was retrieved August 17, 2008 from http://www.medialit.org/pdf/CML_DeconstructionMags.pdf

10. A lesson plan of this activity was retrieved August 17, 2008 from http://medialit.org/reading_room/casestudy/lessons_activities/LP_LorenzaArengoYarnes.pdf

11. Kubey, R., & Baker, F. (1999, October 27). Has media literacy found a curricular foothold? *Education Week.* A map with the state standards that include media literacy was retrieved August 17, 2008 from http://www.frankwbaker.com/state_lit.htm

Chapter Three

1. Two of the biggest media literacy cybergroups based in the U.S. are the ACME E-List with about 700 members and the Media-L listserv sponsored by the Southern New Mexico Media Awareness Council. As of December 29, 2007, the Media-L listserv had 427 members from many parts of the world. You can find information about joining the ACME E-List online. Retrieved August 17, 2008 from http://www.acmecoalition.org/. Information about how to join the Media-L listserv was retrieved August 17, 2008 from http://www.frankwbaker.com/list_serve.htm

2. Retrieved August 17, 2008 from http://www.frankwbaker.com/state_lit.htm

3. Retrieved August 17, 2008 from http://www.mcrel.org/compendium/SubjectTopics.asp?SubjectID=7

4. Susan Saulny writes in the *New York Times* (February 12, 2006) that according to the U.S. Department of Education, of the close to 2 million students eligible for tutoring in 2004, only 12 percent actually received help.

5. For more on these propositions see "The History of Silencing Children" (pp. 87–105) in Santa Ana (2004).

6. In 2005, the Toronto District School Board published *Media Studies K-12*, a theoretical and practical curriculum guide for teaching media literacy. Project leaders: Neil Andersen and Sylvie Webb.

7. Robyn Quin, personal conversation with author at *Summit 2000: Children, Youth and the Media—Beyond the Millennium,* Toronto, Canada, May 13–17, 2000.

8. Retrieved August 17, 2008 from http://www.euromedialiteracy.eu

9. Ediciones de la Torre is in Spanish and is available online. Retrieved August 17, 2008 from http://www.edicionesdelatorre.com/. Books on media education are available in the section Proyecto Didáctico Quirón.

Chapter Four

1. The lesson plans created by SMARTArt teachers retrieved August 17, 2008 from http://www.medialit.org/reading_room/casestudy/lessonsactivities.htm. The guide explaining the theoretical framework that was used for Project SMARTArt retrieved August 17, 2007 from http://www.medialit.org/reading_room/article540.html. The case study with photographs and videos of the 3 years of Project SMARTArt can be seen online at http://www.medialit.org/reading_room/article659.html

2. OCR is an abbreviation for Open Court Reading Program, the district-mandated scripted Language Arts program that all the Leo Politi teachers were required to use.

3. This lesson retrieved August 17, 2008 from http://www.medialit.org/pdf/mlk/02_5KQ_ClassroomGuide.pdf. Look for *http://www.medialit.org/*lesson 2B on p. 31.

4. Manzanar is one of the internment camps that the U.S. government used to lock up Japanese Americans during World War II.

5. More information about the LAUSD Modified Consent Decree can be found online. Retrieved August 18, 2008 from http://dse-web.lausd.k12.ca.us/sepg2s/mcd/mcd.htm

6. The introductory unit and vocabulary unit retrieved August 17, 2008 from http://www.medialit.org/reading_room/casestudy/lessonsactivities.htm

Chapter Five

1. While all people born in this millennium have been alive since the invention of the Internet, cellular phones, and television, this does not mean that everyone can access this technology. Since approximately one third (about 2 billion) of the world's population still live without electricity, it is important to remember that billions of people are being left behind the so-called technological revolution.

2. This data is based on random telephone interviews in 2003 with 1,065 parents of children between 6 months and 6 years of age. "Screen media" refers to watching TV, watching videos/DVDs, using a computer, and playing video games. This research was reported in the Kaiser Family Foundation *Zero to Six* study.

3. The number of hours spent with media is based on questionnaires from a 2004 national sample of 2,032 students between 8 and 18 years of age, as well as 694 media-use diaries, as reported in the Kaiser Family Foundation (2005) *Generation M* study. The figure of 6½ hr per day, includes ¼ of that time spent multitasking with several different media at the same

time, thereby increasing media exposure to an estimated 8½ hr per day.

4. Len Masterman (1994) describes critical autonomy as the ability and desire of students to think critically about media when they are on their own.

5. Critical solidarity, according to Robert Ferguson (2001), involves recognition of the interconnections between people and information as well as empathy to be in solidarity with those marginalized or oppressed by these connections.

6. At 3 years of age, my son was able to explain that advertising was trying to make a product look more fun to trick him to want to buy it.

7. Kathleen Tyner (1998) offers insightful analysis of many types of literacies in *Literacy in a Digital World: Teaching and Learning in the Age of Information*.

8. In spite of this mandate and research supporting the effectiveness of early childhood education, the U.S. is still underfunding these programs. According to an article in *Business Week*, Head Start's "$6.5 billion-a-year budget means it can't accommodate three of five eligible children" (Starr, 2002).

9. Lessons 2A and 2B are photography lessons that I taught these kindergarten students. Retrieved August 18, 2008 from http://www.medialit.org/pdf/mlk/02_5KQ_ClassroomGuide.pdf

10. For 3 years I worked as an occasional substitute teacher in this school and had the opportunity to see how most of the teachers were using technology.

11. The Foxfire *Eleven Core Practices* are available online. Retrieved August 18, 2008 from http://www.foxfire.org/teaching.html

12. The California State Content Standards are available online. Retrieved August 18, 2008 from http://www.cde.ca.gov/be/st/ss/engkindergarten.asp

13. The disruption or denaturalization of media representations is something Robert Ferguson suggests can create a place of liminality or unease that can become productive when teachers and students begin asking "what if" questions about media and society (1998, 2004).

Chapter Six

1. The quote was found on the official UNESCO Web site. Retrieved October 23, 2006, from http://portal.unesco.org/culture/en/ev.php-URL_ID=8270&URL_DO=DO_TOPIC& URL_SECTION=201.html

Bibliography

American Library Association. (2006). *Information literacy competency standards for higher education*. Retrieved August 14, 2006, from http://www.ala.org/acrl/ilcomstan.html

Ang, I. (2002). On the politics of empirical audience research. In M. G. Durham & D. M. Kellner (Eds.), *Media and cultural studies key works* (pp. 177–197). Malden, MA: Blackwell.

Aparici, R. (Ed.). (1997). *La Educación para los Medios de Comunicación*. Mexico: Universidad Pedagógica Nacional.

Bagdikian, B. H. (2004). *The new media monopoly*. Boston: Beacon.

Banks, J. (2000). Series forward. In C. Cortés, *The children are watching: How the media teach about diversity*. New York: Teachers College Press.

Barthes, R. (1998). *Mythologies*. New York: Hill & Wang.

Berger, J. (1977). *Ways of seeing*. London: British Broadcasting Corporation.

Bigelow, B., Christensen, L., Karp, S., Miner, B., & Peterson, B. (Eds.). (1994). *Rethinking our classrooms: Teaching for equity and justice*. Milwaukee, WI: Rethinking Schools.

Bourdieu, P. (1986). The forms of capital. In J. Richardson (Ed.), *Handbook of theory and research for the sociology of education* (pp. 241–258). New York: Greenwood.

Brown, M., & Brown, L. K. (1984). *The Bionic Bunny show*. Boston: Little, Brown.

Buckingham, D. (1994). *Children talking television: The making of television literacy*. London: Falmer.

———. (2000). *After the death of childhood: Growing up in the age of electronic media*. Cambridge, UK: Polity.

———. (2003). *Media education: Literacy, learning and contemporary culture.* Cambridge, UK: Polity.

———. (2005). Constructing the "media competent" child: Media literacy and regulatory policy in the UK. *MedienPädagogik.* Available at: www.medienpaed.com. Accessed January 13, 2006.

Carrington, V. (2005). New textual landscapes, information and early literacy. In J. Marsh (Ed.), *Popular culture, new media and digital literacy in early childhood* (pp. 13–17). London: RoutledgeFalmer.

Castells, M. (2004). *The information age: Economy, society, and culture: The power of identity* (Vol. 2, 2nd ed.). Malden, MA: Blackwell.

Charles, C. M. (2002). *Building classroom discipline* (7th ed.). Boston: Allyn & Bacon.

Collins, P. H. (2000). *Black feminist thought: Knowledge, consciousness, and the politics of empowerment* (2nd ed.). New York: Routledge.

———. (2004). Learning from the outsider within: The sociological significance of black feminist thought. In S. Harding (Ed.), *Feminist standpoint theory reader: Intellectual and political controversies* (pp. 103–126). New York: Routledge.

Colvin, R. L. (2003, October 5). But, teacher, My homework got run over at the taco bell protest. *Los Angeles Times Magazine,* pp. 12–32.

Comber, B. (2001a). Critical literacies and local action: Teacher knowledge and a "new" research agenda. In B. Comber & A. Simpson (Eds.), *Negotiating critical literacies in classrooms* (pp. 271–282). Mahwah, NJ: Lawrence Erlbaum.

———. (2001b). Classroom explorations in critical literacy. In H. Fehring & P. Green (Eds.), *Critical literacy: A collection of articles from the Australian Literacy Educators' Association* (pp. 90–102). Newark, DE: International Reading Association.

Considine, D. (2003). Weapons of mass destruction? Media literacy, social studies and citizenship. In B. Duncan & K. Tyner (Eds.), *Visions/revisions: Moving forward with media education* (pp. 24–45). Madison, WI: National Telemedia Council.

Cortés, C. (2000). *The children are watching: How the media teach about diversity.* New York: Teachers College Press.

Coughlan, S. (2006, September 28). All you need is Ubuntu. *BBC News Magazine.* Retrieved October 27, 2006, from http://news.bbc.co.uk/2/hi/uk_news/magazine/5388182.stm

Couldry, N. (2000). *The palace of media power: Pilgrims and witnesses of the media age.* London and New York: Routledge.

Crawford, P. A. (2004, December). "I follow the blue . . ." A primary teacher and the impact of packaged curricula. *Early Childhood Education Journal, 32*(3), 205–210.

Criticos, C. (1997). Media education for a critical citizenry in South Africa. In R. Kubey (Ed.), *Media literacy in the information age: Current perspectives: Information and behavior* (Vol. 6, pp. 229–240). New Brunswick, NJ: Transaction.

Daley, E. (2003, March/April). Expanding the concept of literacy. *Educause Review,* pp. 33–40. Retrieved August 14, 2006, from http://www.educause.edu/ir/library/pdf/ERM0322.pdf

Darder, A. (1997). Creating the conditions for cultural democracy in the classroom. In A. Darder, R. D. Torres & H. Gutierrez (Eds.), *Latinos and education: A critical reader* (pp. 331–350). New York: Routledge.

Darder, A., Baltodano, M., & Torres, R. (Eds.). (2003). *The critical pedagogy reader.* New York: RoutledgeFalmer.

Debes, J. (1969). The loom of visual literacy. *Audiovisual Instruction, 14*(8), 25–27.

Dewey, J. (1916/1997). *Democracy and education*. New York: Free Press.

———. (1938/1963). *Experience and education*. New York: Collier Books.

Dickinson, D. K. (2002). Shifting images of developmentally appropriate practice as seen through different lenses. *Educational Researcher, 31*(1), 26–32.

Duncan, B., & Tyner, K. (Eds.). (2003). *Visions/revisions: Moving forward with media education*. Madison, WI: National Telemedia Council.

Durham, M. G., & Kellner, D. (Eds.). (2002). *Media and cultural studies: Keyworks*. Malden, MA: Blackwell.

Dyson, A. H. (1997). *Writing superheroes: Contemporary childhood, popular culture, and classroom literacy*. New York: Teachers College Press.

Edelsky, C. (Ed.). (1999). *Making justice our project: Teachers working toward critical whole language practice*. Urbana, IL: NCTE.

Facione, P. A. (1990). *Critical thinking: A statement of expert consensus for purposes of educational assessment and instruction*. Research findings and recommendations prepared for the committee on precollege philosophy of the American Philosophical Association. Retrieved August 13, 2006, from http://www.insightassessment.com/pdf_files/DEXadobe.PDF

Ferguson, R. (1998). *Representing "race": Ideology, identity and the media*. New York: Oxford University Press.

———. (2000, May 13–17). Media education and the development of critical solidarity. CD-ROM with academic papers presented at *Summit 2000: Children youth and the media beyond the millennium*. Toronto, Canada.

———. (2001). Media education and the development of critical solidarity in *Media Education Journal*. Glasgow, Scotland: Association for Media Education in Scotland (AMES) (Vol. 30, pp. 37–43).

———. (2004). *The media in question*. London: Arnold.

Fiske, J. (1990). *Introduction to communication studies* (2nd ed.). London: Routledge.

Flax, J. (1997). Postmodernism and gender relations in feminist theory. In S. Kemp & J. Squires (Eds.), *Feminisms* (pp. 170–178). New York: Oxford University Press.

Foucault, M. (1980). *Power/knowledge: Selected interviews and other writings 1972–1977*. C. Gordon (Ed.). New York: Pantheon Books.

———. (1995). *Discipline and punish: The birth of the prison*. New York: Vintage Books.

Freire, P. (1970). *Pedagogy of the oppressed*. New York: Seabury Press.

Friedman, T. L. (2005). *The world is flat: A brief history of the twenty-first century*. New York: Farrar, Straus & Giroux.

Gee, J. P. (2000). New people in new worlds: Networks, the new capitalism and schools. In B. Cope & M. Kalantzis (Eds.), *Multiliteracies: Literacy, learning and the design of social futures* (pp. 43–68). Melbourne, Australia: Macmillan.

Geist, E., & Baum, A. C. (2005). Yeah, but's that keep teachers from embracing an active curriculum: Overcoming the resistance. *Beyond the journal. Journal of the National Association for the Education of Young Children*. Retrieved August 10, 2006, from http://www.journal.naeyc.org/btj/200507/03Geist.pdf

Giroux, H. (1987). Introduction. In P. Freire & D. Macedo (Eds.), *Literacy: Reading the word and the world* (pp. 1–27). Westport, CT: Bergin & Garvey.

———. (1997). *Pedagogy of the politics of hope: Theory, culture, and schooling*. Boulder, CO: Westview.

———. (1999). *The mouse that roared: Disney and the end of innocence*. Boulder, CO: Rowman &

Littlefield.

———. (2001). *Theory and resistance in education: Towards a pedagogy for the opposition.* Westport, CT: Bergin & Garvey.

Goodman, S. (2003). *Teaching youth media: A critical guide to literacy, video production, and social change.* New York: Teachers College Press.

Gutiérrez, M. A. (2003). Multimedia authoring as a fundamental principle of literacy and teacher training in the information age. In B. Duncan & K. Tyner (Eds.), *Visions/revisions: Moving forward with media education* (pp. 12–22). Madison, WI: National Telemedia Council.

Hall, K. (1998). Critical literacy and the case for it in the early years of school. *Language, Culture and Curriculum, 11*(2), 183–194.

Hall, S. (1980). Encoding/decoding. In S. Hall, D. Hobson, A. Lowe & P. Willis (Eds.), *Culture, media, language: Working papers in cultural studies 1972–1979* (pp. 128–138). London: Hutchinson.

———. (2003). The whites of their eyes: Racist ideologies and the media. In G. Dines & J. M. Humez (Eds.), *Gender, race, and class in media* (2nd ed., pp. 89–93). Thousand Oaks, CA: Sage.

Hammer, R. (2006). Teaching critical media literacies: Theory, praxis and empowerment. *InterActions: UCLA Journal of Education and Information Studies, 2*(1). Retrieved February 17, 2006, from http://repositories.cdlib.org/gseis/interactions/vol2/iss1/art7/

Harding, S. (1998). *Is science multicultural? Postcolonialisms, feminisms, and epistemologies.* Bloomington: Indiana University Press.

———. (Ed.). (2004). Introduction: Standpoint theory as a site of political, philosophic, and scientific debate. In S. Harding (Ed.), *Feminist standpoint theory reader: Intellectual and political controversies* (pp. 1–15). New York: Routledge.

Hart, A. (Ed.). (1998). *Teaching the media: International perspectives.* Mahwah, NJ: Lawrence Erlbaum.

Hartsock, N. (1997). The feminist standpoint: Developing the ground for a specifically feminist historical materialism. In S. Kemp & J. Squires (Eds.), *Feminisms* (pp. 152–160). New York: Oxford University Press.

Hemphill, C. (2006, July 26). In kindergarten playtime, a new meaning for "play." *The New York Times.* Retrieved August 2, 2006, from http://www.nytimes.com/2006/07/26/education/26education.html?_r=1&oref=slogin

Hobbs, R. (1998). The seven great debates in the media literacy movement. *Journal of Communication, 48*(1), 16–32.

hooks, b. (1994). *Teaching to transgress.* New York: Routledge.

———. (1996). *Reel to real: Race, sex, and class at the movies.* New York: Routledge.

———. (2004). Choosing the margin as a space of radical openness. In S. Harding (Ed.), *Feminist standpoint theory reader: Intellectual and political controversies* (pp. 153–159). New York: Routledge.

Horkheimer, M., & Adorno, T. (2002). *Dialectic of enlightenment.* Palo Alto, CA: Stanford University Press.

Houston, B. (1984). Viewing television: The metapsychology of endless consumption. *Quarterly Review of Film Studies, 9*(3), 183–195.

International Reading Association (IRA) and National Association for the Education of Young Children (NAEYC). (1998, July). Learning to read and write: Developmentally appropriate practices for young children. A joint position statement of the International Reading

Association and the National Association for the Education of Young Children. *Young Children, 53*(4), 30–46. Retrieved August 13, 2006, from www.naeyc.org/about/positions/pdf/PSREAD98.PDF

Jenkins, H. (2006). *Convergence culture: Where old and new media collide.* New York: New York University Press.

Jenkins, H., Purushotma, R., Clinton, K. Weigel, M., & Robison, A. J. (2007). *Confronting the challenges of participatory culture: Media education for the 21st century.* Retrieved December 1, 2007, from http://www.projectnml.org/files/working/NMLWhitePaper.pdf

Kaiser Family Foundation. (March 9, 2005). *Generation M: Media in the lives of 8–18 year-olds.* (Publication No. 7250). Retrieved May 14, 2005, from http://www.kff.org/entmedia/entmedia030905pkg.cfm

Kanner, A. D. (2006). The corporatized child. *Independent Practitioner: Bulletin of Psychologists in Independent Practice, 26*(3), 135–136.

Kaplún, M. (1998). *Una Pedagogía de la Comunicación.* Madrid: Ediciones de la Torre.

Kapur, J. (1999). Out of control: Television and the transformation of childhood in late capitalism. In M. Kinder (Ed.), *Kids' media culture.* Durham, NC, and London: Duke University Press.

Kellner, D. (1995). *Media culture: Cultural studies, identity and politics between the modern and the postmodern.* New York: Routledge.

———. (1998). Multiple literacies and critical pedagogy in a multicultural society. *Educational Theory, 48*(1), 103–122.

———. (2004). Technological transformation, multiple literacies, and the re-visioning of education. In *E-Learning, 1*(1), (pp. 9-37).

———. (2006a). Technological transformation, multiple literacies, and the re-visioning of education. In J. Weiss, J. Nolan, J. Hunsinger & P. Trifonas (Eds.), *The international handbook of virtual learning environments* (Vol. 1, pp. 241–268). Dordrecht, the Netherlands: Springer.

———. (2006b). *Media culture and the triumph of the spectacle.* Retrieved October 12, 2006, from http://www.gseis.ucla.edu/faculty/kellner/papers/medculturespectacle.html

Kellner, D., & Share, J. (2005). Toward critical media literacy: Core concepts, debates, organizations and policy. *Discourse: Studies in the Cultural Politics of Education, 26*(3), pp. 369–386.

———. (2007). Critical media literacy, democracy, and the reconstruction of education. In D. Macedo & S. R. Steinberg (Eds.), *Media literacy: A reader* (pp. 3–23). New York: Peter Lang.

Kemp, S., & Squires, J. (Eds.). (1997). *Feminisms.* New York: Oxford University Press.

Kincheloe, J. (2004). McDonald's, power and children: Ronald McDonald/Ray Kroc does it all for you. In S. Steinberg & J. Kincheloe (Eds.), *Kinderculture: The corporate construction of childhood* (2nd ed., pp. 120–149). Boulder, CO: Westview.

Kinder, M. (1991). *Playing with power in movies, television, and video games.* Berkeley: University of California Press.

Kist, W. (2005). *New literacies in action: Teaching and learning in multiple media.* New York: Teachers College Press.

Klein, N. (2007). The shock doctrine: The rise of disaster capitalism. New York: Metropolitan Books.

Kozol, J. (2005). *The shame of the nation: The restoration of apartheid schooling in America.* New York: Crown Publishers.

Krashen, S. (1995). Bilingual education and second language acquisition theory. In D. Durkin

(Ed.), *Language Issues: Readings for Teachers* (pp. 90–116). White Plains, NY: Longman.

Kress, G. (2004). *Literacy in the new media age*. New York: Routledge.

Kubey, R., & Baker, F. (1999, October 27). Has media literacy found a curricular foothold? *Education Week, 19*(9), 38, 56.

Lealand, G. (2003). From the margins come great things: Media teaching in New Zealand. In B. Duncan & K. Tyner (Eds.), *Visions/revisions: Moving forward with media education* (pp. 142–148). Madison, WI: National Telemedia Council.

Lee, A.Y.L. (2003). "The Media Education Network in Hong Kong and key trends of world communication." In Duncan, B., & Tyner, K. (Eds.), *Visions / revisions: Moving forward with media education*. Madison, WI: National Telemedia Council. (pp. 149–158).

Lemish, D., & Lemish, P. (1997). A much debated consensus: Media literacy in Israel. In R. Kubey (Ed.), *Media literacy in the information age: Current perspectives: Information and behavior* (Vol. 6, pp. 213–228). New Brunswick, NJ: Transaction.

Lo Bianco, J. (2000). Multiliteracies and multilingualism. In B. Cope & M. Kalantzis (Eds.), *Multiliteracies: Literacy, learning and the design of social futures* (pp. 92–105). Melbourne, Australia: Macmillan.

Luke, A. (2000, February). Critical literacy in Australia: A matter of context and standpoint. *Journal of Adolescent and Adult Literacy, 43*(5), 448–461.

Luke, A., & Freebody, P. (1997). Shaping the social practices of reading. In S. Muspratt, A. Luke & P. Freebody (Eds.), *Constructing critical literacies: Teaching and learning textual practice* (pp. 185–225). Sydney: Allen & Unwin, and Cresskill, NJ: Hampton Press.

———. (1999). Further notes on the four resources model. *Reading Online.* Retrieved February 12, 2006, from http://www.readingonline.org/research/lukefreebody.html

Luke, C. (1990). *TV and your child*. Sydney: Angus & Robertson.

———. (1994, Summer). Feminist pedagogy and critical media literacy. *Journal of Communication Inquiry, 18*(2), pp. 30–47.

———. (1997). *Technological literacy*. Melbourne, Australia: National Languages & Literacy Institute.

———. (1999, May). Media and cultural studies in Australia. *Journal of Adolescent and Adult Literacy, 42*(8), 622–626.

———. (2000a, February). New literacies in teacher education. *Journal of Adolescent and Adult Literacy, 43*(5), 424–436.

———. (2000b). Cyber-schooling and technological change: Multiliteracies for new times. In B. Cope & M. Kalantzis (Eds.), *Multiliteracies: Literacy, learning and the design of social futures* (pp. 69–105). Melbourne, Australia: Macmillan.

———. (2004). Re-crafting media and ICT literacies. In D. E. Alvermann (Ed.), *Adolescents and literacies in a digital world* (pp. 132–146). New York: Peter Lang.

———. (2006). Cyberpedagogy. In J. Weiss, J. Nolan, J. Hunsinger & P. Trifonas (Eds.), *The international handbook of virtual learning environments* (Vol. 1, pp. 269–278). Dordrecht, the Netherlands: Springer.

———. (2007). As seen on TV or was that my phone? *New media* literacy. *Policy Futures in Education, 5*(1), 50–58. Online-only journal published by *Symposium Journals*. Retrieved from http://www.wwwords.co.uk/pfie/

Marcuse, H. (1991). *One-dimensional man: Studies in the ideology of advanced industrial society*. Boston: Beacon Press.

Marsh, J., Brooks, G., Hughes, J., Ritchie, L., Roberts, S., & Wright, K. (2005). *Digital begin-*

nings: Young children's use of popular culture, media and new technologies. University of Sheffield: Literacy Research Centre. Retrieved September 6, 2006, from http://www.digitalbeginnings.shef.ac.uk/DigitalBeginningsReport.pdf

Masterman, L. (1985/2001). *Teaching the media.* New York: Routledge.

———. (1994). A rationale for media education (Part I). In L. Masterman & F. Mariet (Eds.), *Media education in 1990s' Europe* (pp. 5–87). Strasbourg, France: Council of Europe.

———. (1996). Media education and human rights. *Continuum: The Australian Journal of Media and Culture, 9*(2), 74–77.

McChesney, R. (1999, November 29). The new global media: It's a small world of big conglomerates [Special issue]. *The Nation, 269*(18), 11–15.

———. (2003). *The nine firms that dominate the world.* New York: Global Policy Forum. Retrieved August 16, 2008, http://www.globalpolicy.org/globaliz/cultural/2003/0804media.htm

———. (2004). *The problem of the media: U.S. communication politics in the 21st century.* New York: Monthly Review Press.

McClure, C. R. (1993). Network literacy in an electronic society: An educational disconnect? In *The knowledge economy: The nature of information in the 21st century* (pp. 137–178). Queenstown, MD: Aspen Institute.

McLuhan, M. (1997). *Understanding media: Extensions of man.* Cambridge, MA: MIT Press.

McMahon, B. (1996). Resharpening the edge: The educational riddle. *Continuum: The Australian Journal of Media and Culture, 9*(2), 161–171.

Mercer, N. (2007). *Words and minds: How we use language to think together.* London: Routledge.

Miller, E. (2005, November). Fighting technology for toddlers. *Education Digest, 71*(3), 55–58.

Ministry of Education. (1989). *Media literacy: Intermediate and senior divisions, 1989.* Ontario, Canada: Ministry of Education.

Mission, R., & Morgan, W. (2006). *Critical literacy and the aesthetic: Transforming the English classroom.* Urbana, IL: NCTE.

Mizukoshi, S., & Yamauchi, Y. (2003). Perspectives on Japan's media environment and the MELL Project. In B. Duncan & K. Tyner (Eds.), *Visions/revisions: Moving forward with media education* (pp. 159–178). Madison, WI: National Telemedia Council.

Modleski, T. (1982). *Loving with a vengeance: Mass produced fantasies for women.* New York: Routledge.

Morduchowicz, R. (2003). Media education is education for democracy. In B. Duncan & K. Tyner (Eds.), *Visions/revisions: Moving forward with media education* (pp. 64–71). Madison, WI: National Telemedia Council.

Narayan, U. (2004). The project of feminist epistemology: Perspectives from a nonwestern feminist. In S. Harding (Ed.), *Feminist standpoint theory reader: Intellectual and political controversies* (pp. 213–224). New York: Routledge.

National Council of Teachers of English (NCTE) and International Reading Association (IRA). (1996). *Standards for the English language arts.* NCTE Urbana, Il. & IRA Newark, DE.

Neuman, S., & Roskos, K. (2005a, Second Quarter). The state of state pre-kindergarten standards. *Early Childhood Research Quarterly, 20*(2), 125–145.

———. (2005b, July). Whatever happened to developmentally appropriate practice in early literacy? *Beyond the journal. Journal of the National Association for the Education of Young Children.* Retrieved August 10, 2006, from http://www.journal.naeyc.org/btj/200507/02Neuman.pdf

Newcomb, H., & Hirsch, P. M. (1994). Television as a cultural forum. In H. Newcomb (Ed.). (5th ed.). *Television: The critical view* (pp. 503–515). New York: Oxford University Press. Originally published in *Quarterly Review of Film Studies,* Summer 1983.

The New London Group. (1996). A pedagogy of multiliteracies: Designing social futures. *Harvard Educational Review, 66*(1), 60–92.

Nicoll, B. (1996, January). *Developing minds: Critical thinking in K–3.* Paper presented at the California Kindergarten Conference, San Francisco, CA.

O'Connor, A. (2006). *Raymond Williams.* New York: Rowman & Littlefield.

O'Sullivan, T., Hartley, J., Saunders, D., Montgomery, M., & Fiske, J. (1995). *Key concepts in communication and cultural studies* (2nd ed.). London: Routledge.

Postman, N. (1985). *Amusing ourselves to death: Public discourse in the age of show business.* New York: Penguin Books.

Prinsloo, J., & Criticos, C. (Eds.). (1991). *Media matters in South Africa.* Durban, South Africa: Media Resource Centre.

Pungente, J., & O'Malley, M. (1999). *More than meets the eye: Watching television watching us.* Toronto, Canada: McClelland & Stewart.

Pungente, J., Duncan, B., & Andersen, N. (2005). The Canadian experience: Leading the way. In G. Schwarz & P. U. Brown (Eds.), *Media literacy: Transforming curriculum and teaching* (pp. 140–160). *The 104th yearbook of the National Society for the Study of Education* (Part I). Malden, MA: Blackwell Publishing.

Quin, R., & McMahon, B. (2003). Relevance and rigour in media education: A path to reflection on our identity. In B. Duncan & K. Tyner (Eds.), *Visions/revisions: Moving forward with media education* (pp. 122–140). Madison, WI: National Telemedia Council.

Raffi. (1992). *Baby Beluga.* Toronto, Canada: Crown.

Rideout, V., Roberts, D. F., & Foehr, U. G. (2005). *Generation M: Media in the lives of 8–18 year-olds.* Washington, DC: Kaiser Family Foundation. Retrieved August 18, 2008 from http://www.kff.org/entmedia/entmedia030905pkg.cfm

Rideout, V. J., Vandewater, E. A., & Wartella, E. A. (2003). *Zero to six: Electronic media in the lives of infants, toddlers and preschoolers.* Washington, DC: Kaiser Family Foundation. Retrieved August 18, 2008 from http://www.kff.org/entmedia/3378.cfm

Robins, K., & Webster, F. (2001). *Times of the technoculture.* New York: Routledge.

Robson, J., Simmons, J. and Sohn-Rethel, M. (1990) 'Implementing a media education policy across the curriculum', in Buckingham, D. (ed.) *Watching media Learning: Making Sense of Media Education* London: Falmer.

Rogoff, B., & Morelli, G. (1989, February). Perspectives on children's development from cultural psychology. *American Psychologist, 44*(2), 343–348.

Rogow, F. (2004, September). Shifting from media to literacy: One opinion on the challenges of media literacy education. *American Behavioral Scientist, 48*(1), 30–34.

Santa Ana, O. (Ed.). (2004). Tongue-tied: The lives of multilingual children in public education. New York: Rowman & Littlefield.

Saulny, S. (2006, February 12). Tutor program offered by law is going unused. *The New York Times,* Retrieved August 18, 2008 from http://www.nytimes.com/2006/02/12/education/12tutor.html

Seiter, E. (2002). *Television and new media audiences.* New York: Oxford University Press.

———. (2004, May). Children reporting online: The cultural politics of the computer lab. *Television and New Media, 5*(2), 87–107.

Share, J. (2005). *Five key questions that can change the world: Classroom activities for media literacy.* Center for Media Literacy. Retrieved August 17, 2008 from http://www.medialit.org/pdf/mlk/02_5KQ_ClassroomGuide.pdf

Share, J., & Thoman, E. (2007). *Teaching democracy: A media literacy approach.* Los Angeles: National Center for the Preservation of Democracy. Retrieved August 17, 2008 from http://www.ncdemocracy.org/sites/www.ncdemocracy.org/files/docs/D+Dweb_educators_guide.pdf

Silverblatt, A., Baker, F., Tyner, K., & Stuhlman, L. (2002). *Media literacy in U.S. institutions of higher education.* Retrieved March 20, 2005, from http://www.webster.edu/medialiteracy/survey/survey_Report.htm

Starr, A. (2002, April 29). Does universal preschool pay?. *BusinessWeek.* Retrieved August 14, 2006 from http://www.businessweek.com/magazine/content/02_17/b3780100.htm?chan=search

Steinberg, S., & Kincheloe, J. (Eds.). (2004). *Kinderculture: The corporate construction of childhood* (2nd ed.). Boulder, CO: Westview.

Thomas, L. G., & Knezek, D. G. (1995). *Technology literacy for the nation and for its citizens.* Technology Literacy White Paper. Retrieved August 14, 2006, from the International Society for Technology in Education (ISTE) Web site: http://www.iste.org/Content/NavigationMenu/Research/Reports/Technology_Literacy_White_Paper_1995_/Technology_Literacy_for_the_Nation_and_for_Its_Citizens.htm

Turkle, S. (1997). *Life on the screen: Identity in the age of the Internet.* New York: Touchstone.

Tyner, K. (1998). *Literacy in a digital world: Teaching and learning in the age of information.* Mahwah, NJ: Lawrence Erlbaum.

Tyre, P. (2006, September 11). The new first grade: Too much too soon? *Newsweek Magazine.* Retrieved September 6, 2006, from http://msnbc.msn.com/id/14638573/site/newsweek/

Valencia, R., & Solorzano, D. (2004), Today's deficit thinking about the education of minority students. In O. Santa Ana (Ed.), *Tongue-tied: The lives of multilingual children in public education* (pp. 124–133). New York: Rowman & Littlefield.

Vasquez, V. (2003). *Getting beyond "I like the book": Creating space for critical literacy in K-6 classrooms.* Newark, DE: International Reading Association.

———. (2004). *Negotiating critical literacies with young children.* Mahwah, NJ: Lawrence Erlbaum.

Wiggins, G., & McTighe, J. (2001). *Understanding by design.* Upper Saddle River, NJ: Prentice Hall.

Wittig, M. (1997). One is not born a woman. In S. Kemp & J. Squires (Eds.), *Feminisms* (pp. 220–226). New York: Oxford University Press.

Zemelman, S., Daniels, H., & Hyde, A. (1993). *Best practice: New standards for teaching and learning in America's schools.* Portsmouth, NH: Heinemann.

Zinn, H. (1990). *The politics of history* (2nd ed.). Urbana: University of Illinois Press.

About the Author

Jeff Share worked for ten years as a freelance photojournalist documenting situations of poverty and social activism on several continents. He spent six years teaching bilingual primary school in the Los Angeles Unified School District. After working as the Regional Coordinator for Training at the Center for Media Literacy, Share earned his Ph.D. in the Graduate School of Education and Information Studies at UCLA. His current research and practice focuses on the teaching of critical media literacy in K–12 education. He is currently a faculty advisor in the Teacher Education Program at UCLA.

RETHINKING CHILDHOOD

JOE L. KINCHELOE & GAILE CANNELLA, *General Editors*

A revolution is occurring regarding the study of childhood. Traditional notions of child development are under attack, as are the methods by which children are studied. At the same time, the nature of childhood itself is changing as children gain access to information once reserved for adults only. Technological innovations, media, and electronic information have narrowed the distinction between adults and children, forcing educators to rethink the world of schooling in this new context.

This series of textbooks and monographs encourages scholarship in all of these areas, eliciting critical investigations in developmental psychology, early childhood education, multicultural education, and cultural studies of childhood.

Proposals and manuscripts may be sent to the general editors:

> Joe L. Kincheloe
> c/o Peter Lang Publishing, Inc.
> 29 Broadway, 18th floor
> New York, New York 10006

To order other books in this series, please contact our Customer Service Department at:

> (800) 770-LANG (within the U.S.)
> (212) 647-7706 (outside the U.S.)
> (212) 647-7707 FAX

Or browse online by series at:
> www.peterlang.com